EASY GUITAR
WITH NOTES & TAB

FOLK POP SONGS

ISBN: 978-1-4950-9012-7

HAL•LEONARD®

Visit Hal Leonard Online at
www.halleonard.com

Contact Us:
Hal Leonard
7777 West Bluemound Road
Milwaukee, WI 53213
Email: info@halleonard.com

In Europe contact:
Hal Leonard Europe Limited
Distribution Centre, Newmarket Road
Bury St Edmunds, Suffolk, IP33 3YB
Email: info@halleonardeurope.com

In Australia contact:
Hal Leonard Australia Pty. Ltd.
4 Lentara Court
Cheltenham, Victoria, 3192 Australia
Email: info@halleonard.com.au

STRUM AND PICK PATTERNS

This chart contains the suggested strum and pick patterns that are referred to by number at the beginning of each song in this book. The symbols ⊓ and ∨ in the strum patterns refer to down and up strokes, respectively. The letters in the pick patterns indicate which right-hand fingers play which strings.

p = thumb
i = index finger
m = middle finger
a = ring finger

For example; Pick Pattern 2
is played: thumb - index - middle - ring

You can use the 3/4 Strum and Pick Patterns in songs written in compound meter (6/8, 9/8, 12/8, etc.). For example, you can accompany a song in 6/8 by playing the 3/4 pattern twice in each measure. The 4/4 Strum and Pick Patterns can be used for songs written in cut time (¢) by doubling the note time values in the patterns. Each pattern would therefore last two measures in cut time.

Alison

Words and Music by Elvis Costello

Strum Pattern: 3, 4
Pick Pattern: 6

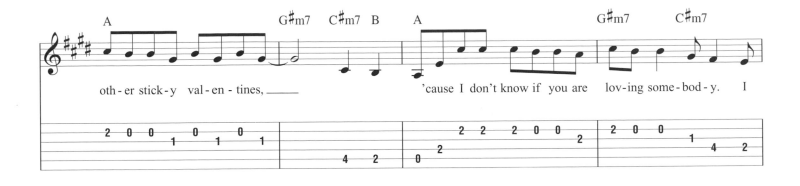

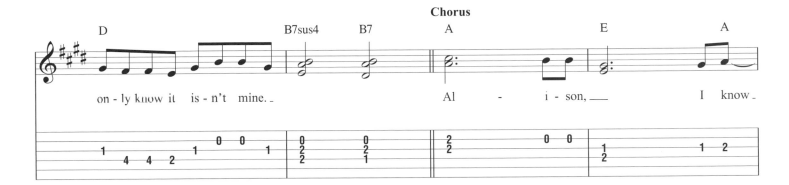

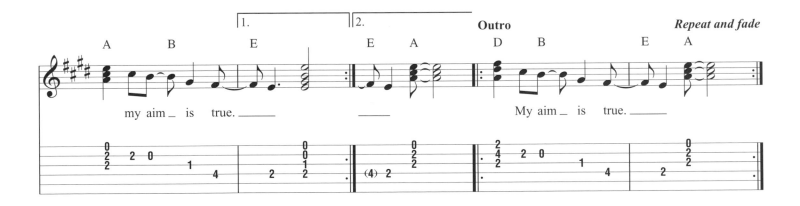

Additional Lyrics

2. Well, I see you got a husband now.
   Did he leave your pretty fingers lying in the wedding cake?
   You used to hold him right in your hand.

   I'll bet he took all he could take.
   Sometimes I wish that I could stop you from talking
   When I hear the silly things that you say.

   I think somebody better put out the big light,
   'Cause I can't stand to see you this way.

American Pie

Words and Music by Don McLean

*One strum per chord throughout Intro

with ev - 'ry pa - per I'd de - liv - er. Bad news on the door - step, I could-n't take one more step. I

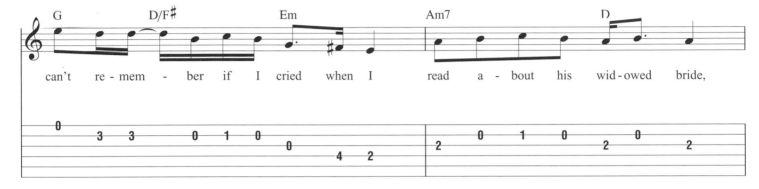

can't re - mem - ber if I cried when I read a - bout his wid - owed bride,

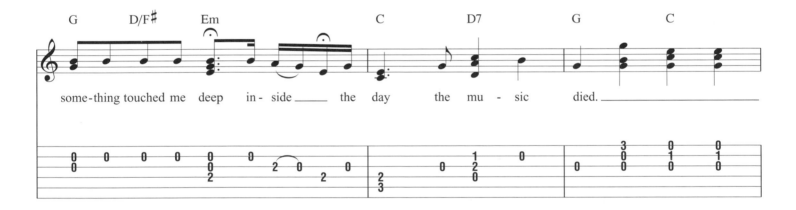

some - thing touched me deep in - side ____ the day the mu - sic died. _____

Strum Pattern: 2
Pick pattern: 2
Chorus
***Moderately**

____ So bye - bye Miss A - mer - i - can Pie, __ drove my Chev - y to the lev - ee but the

*1st time
2. – 4. times, Moderately fast

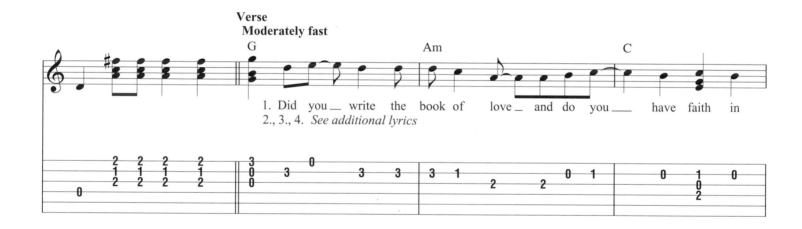

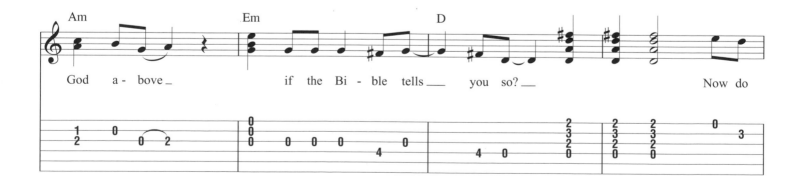

*One strum per chord (next 18 meas.)

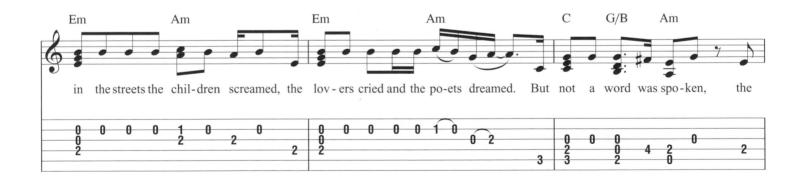

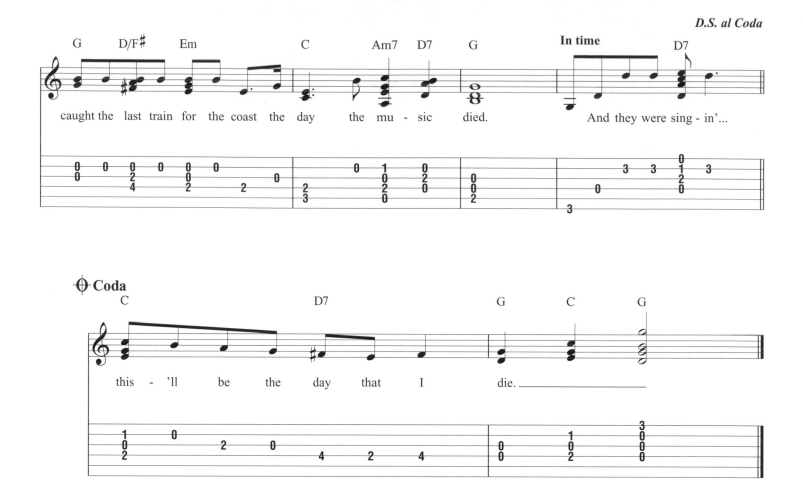

caught the last train for the coast the day the mu - sic died. And they were sing - in'...

Coda

this - 'll be the day that I die. _____

Additional Lyrics

2. Now for ten years we've been on our own, and moss grows fat on a rollin' stone.
   But, that's not how it used to be.
   When the jester sang for the king and queen in a coat he borrowed from James Dean.
   And a voice that came from you and me.
   Oh, and while the king was looking down, the jester stole his thorny crown.
   The courtroom was adjourned, no verdict was returned.
   And while Lenin read a book on Marx, a quartet practiced in the park.
   And we sang dirges in the dark, the day the music died.
   We were singin'...

3. Helter-skelter in the summer swelter, the birds flew off with a fallout shelter,
   Eight miles high and fallin' fast.
   It landed foul on the grass. The players tried for a forward pass,
   With the jester on the sidelines in a cast.
   Now, the half-time air was sweet perfume, while the sergeants played a marching tune.
   We all got up to dance, oh, but we never got the chance.
   'Cause the players tried to take the field, the marching band refused to yield.
   Do you recall what was revealed the day the music died?
   We started singin'...

4. Oh, and there we were all in one place, a generation lost in space,
   With no time left to start again.
   So, come on, Jack be nimble, Jack be quick. Jack Flash sat on a candlestick,
   'Cause fire is the devil's only friend.
   Oh, and as I watched him on the stage my hands were clenched in fists of rage.
   No angel born in hell could break that Satan's spell.
   And as the flames climbed high into the night to light the sacrificial rite,
   I saw Satan laughing with delight, the day the music died.
   He was singin'...

Aquarius

from the Broadway Musical Production HAIR

Words by James Rado and Gerome Ragni
Music by Galt MacDermot

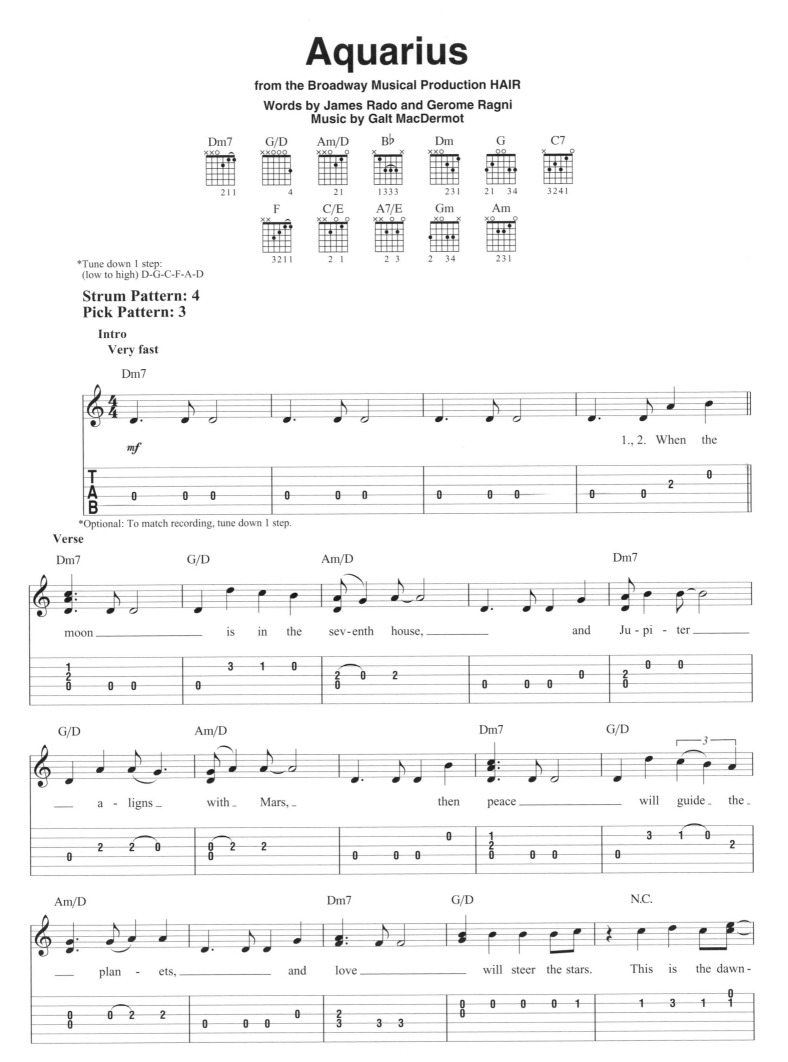

*Tune down 1 step:
(low to high) D-G-C-F-A-D

Strum Pattern: 4
Pick Pattern: 3

Intro
Very fast

*Optional: To match recording, tune down 1 step.

Chorus

-ing of the age of A - quar - i - us, ___ age of A - quar - i - us. ___

A - quar - i - us. ___

To Coda ⊕

A - quar - i - us. ___

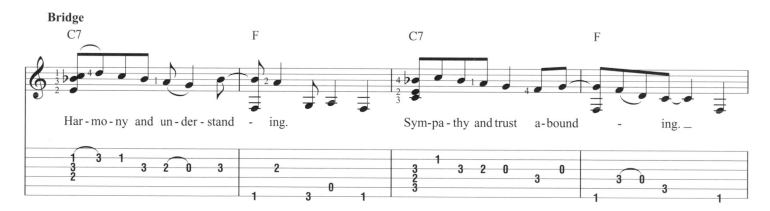

Bridge

Har - mo - ny and un - der - stand - ing. Sym - pa - thy and trust a - bound - ing. ___

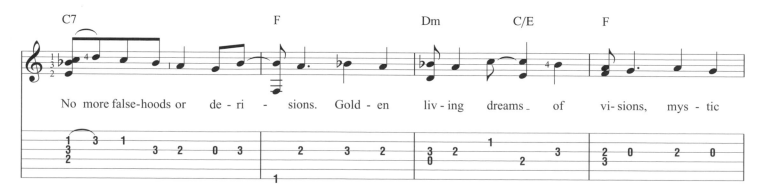

No more false - hoods or de - ri - sions. Gold - en liv - ing dreams ___ of vi - sions, mys - tic

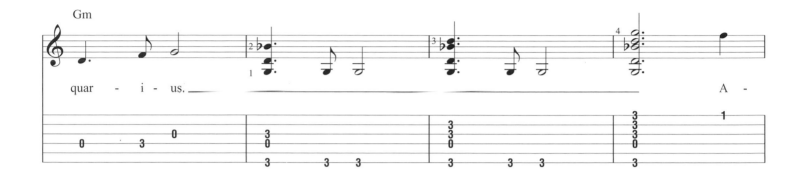

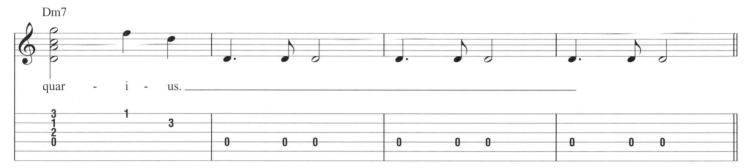

D.C. al Coda

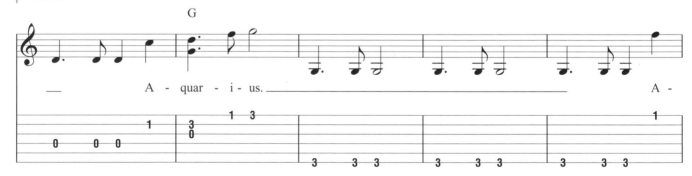

Coda

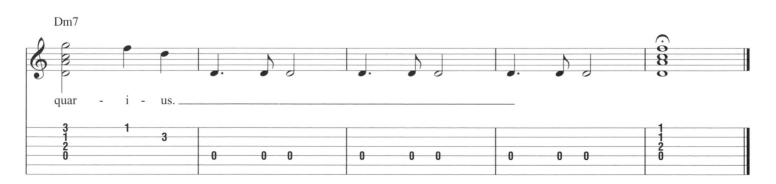

Big Yellow Taxi

Words and Music by Joni Mitchell

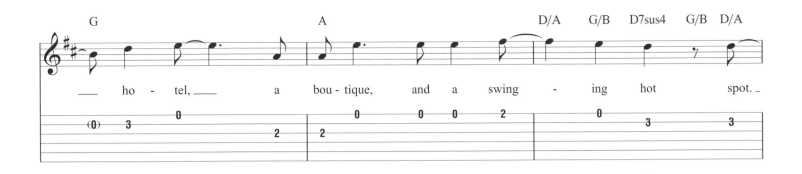

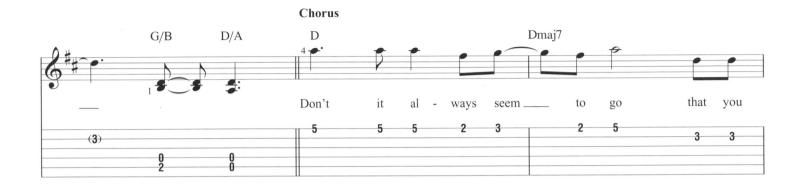

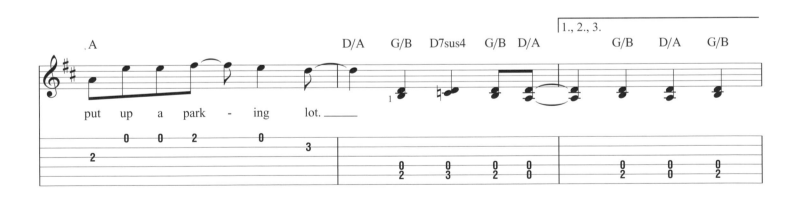

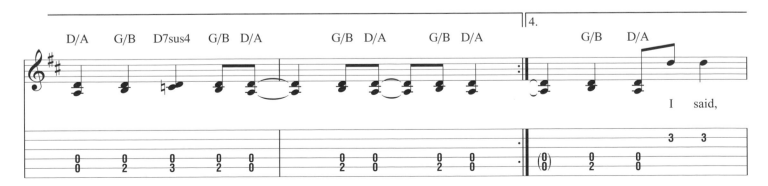

don't it al - ways seem ___ to go that you don't know what ___ you've got ___

Outro

___ 'til it's gone? They paved par - a - dise, put up a park - ing lot. ___

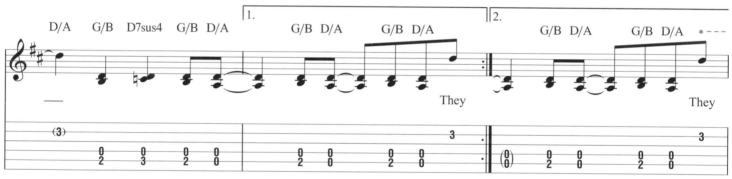

They

They

*Sung one octave higher.

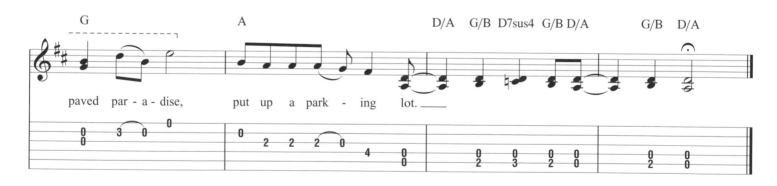

paved par - a - dise, put up a park - ing lot. ___

Additional Lyrics

2. They took all the trees, put 'em in a tree museum,
   And they charged the people a dollar and half just to see 'em.

3. Hey, farmer, farmer, put away that DDT now,
   Give me spots on my apples, but leave me the birds and the bees, please.

4. Late last night, I heard the screen door slam,
   And a big, yellow taxi took away my old man.

Casey Jones

Words by Robert Hunter
Music by Jerry Garcia

Verse

1. This old en - gine makes it on time, __ leaves Cen - tral Sta - tion 'bout a
2., 4. *See additional lyrics*
3. *Instrumental*

quar - ter to nine. __ Hits Riv - er Junc - tion at sev - en - teen to. __ At a

𝄋 **Chorus**

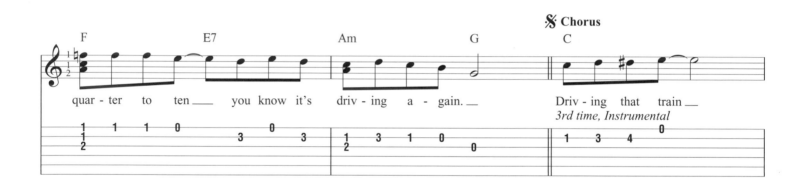

quar - ter to ten __ you know it's driv - ing a - gain. __ Driv - ing that train __
3rd time, Instrumental

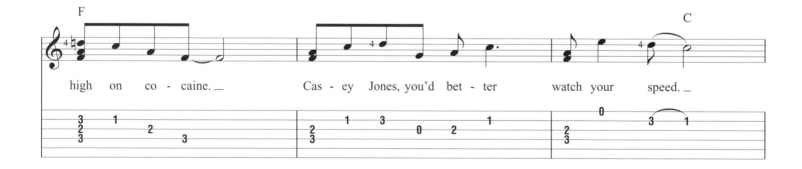

high on co - caine. __ Cas - ey Jones, you'd bet - ter watch your speed. __

5th time, To Coda ⊕

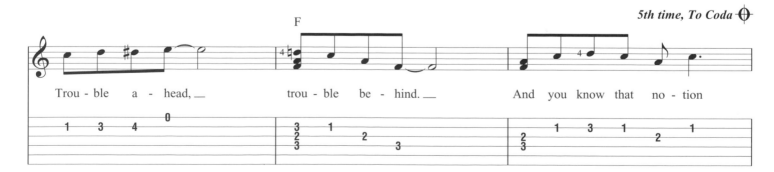

Trou - ble a - head, __ trou - ble be - hind. __ And you know that no - tion

just crossed my mind.
Instrumental ends

4.

D.S. al Coda

just crossed my mind.

Coda

just crossed my mind.

Chorus

Driv-ing that train

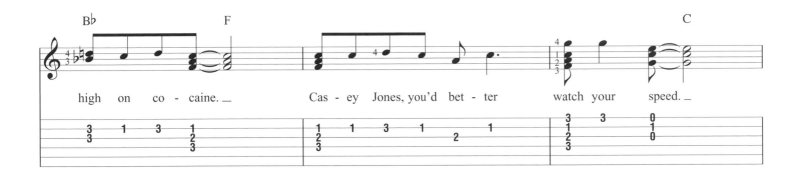

high on co-caine. Cas-ey Jones, you'd bet-ter watch your speed.

Trou-ble a-head, trou-ble be-hind. And you know that no-tion

just crossed my mind. just crossed my mind. And you know that no-tion just crossed my mind.

Additional Lyrics

2. Trouble ahead, the lady in red.
   Take my advice, you'd be better off dead.
   Switchman's sleeping, train hundred and two
   Is on the wrong track and headed for you.

4. Trouble with you is the trouble with me.
   Got two good eyes but we still don't see.
   Come 'round the bend, you know it's the end.
   The fireman screams and the engine just gleams.

California Dreamin'

Words and Music by John Phillips and Michelle Phillips

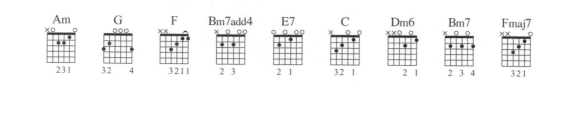

Strum Pattern: 3, 6
Pick Pattern: 3, 5

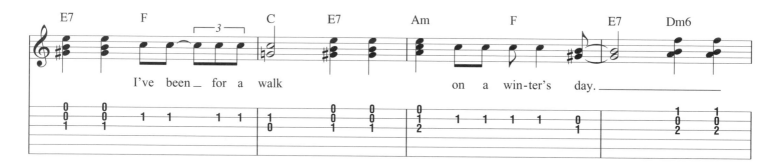

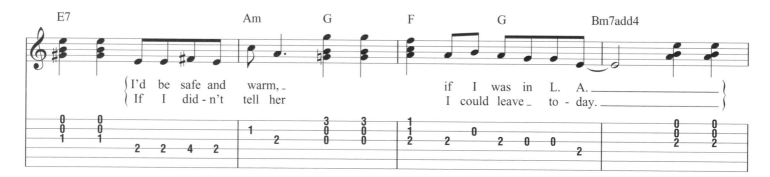

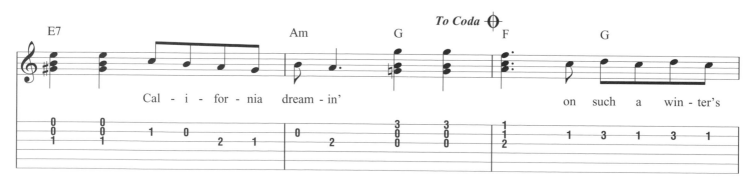

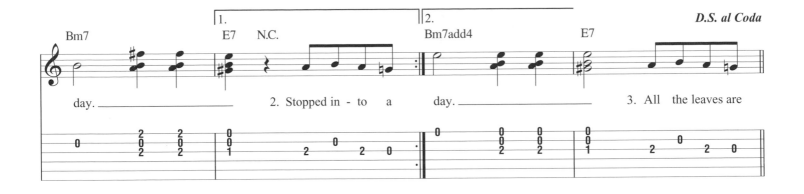

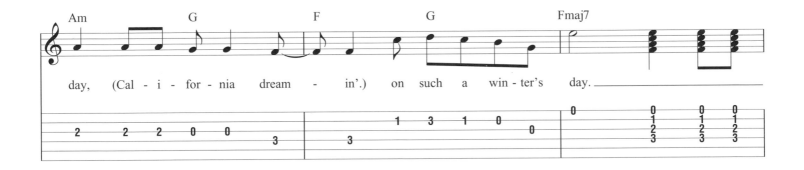

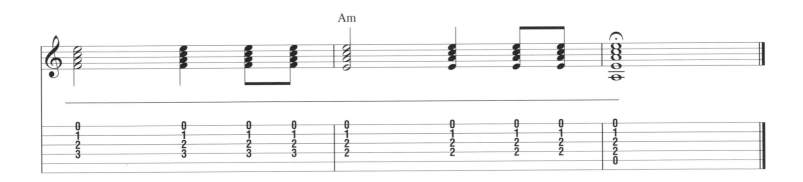

Additional Lyrics

2. Stopped into a church I passed along the way.
   Oh, I got down on my knees, and I pretend to pray.
   You know the preacher, like the cold, he knows I'm gonna stay.
   California dreamin', on such a winter's day.

Cat's in the Cradle

Words and Music by Harry Chapin and Sandy Chapin

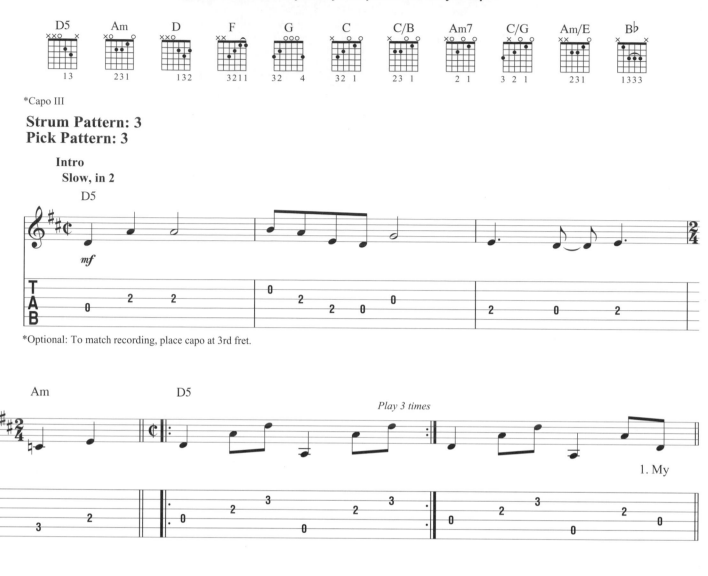

*Capo III

Strum Pattern: 3
Pick Pattern: 3

Intro
   Slow, in 2

*Optional: To match recording, place capo at 3rd fret.

Play 3 times

1. My

Verse

child ar-rived____ just the oth-er day;____ he came to the world in the
2. *See additional lyrics*

u-su-al way.____ But there were planes to catch____ and bills to pay;____

we'll get to - geth - er then, _____ { 3. Dad, } you know we'll have a good time then."

Interlude

1.   2.

2. My   3. Well, he

Verse

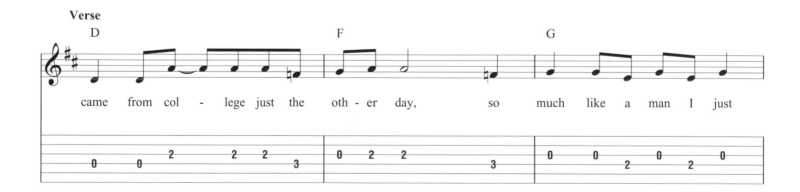

came from col - lege just the oth - er day, so much like a man I just

had to say, _____ "Son, I'm proud of you. _____ Can you sit for a while?" _ He

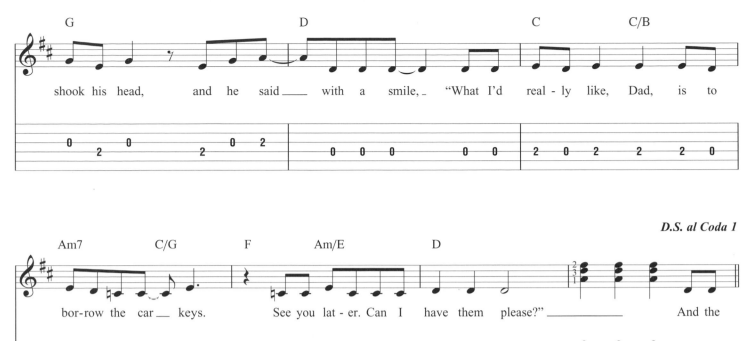

shook his head, and he said___ with a smile, _ "What I'd real-ly like, Dad, is to

D.S. al Coda 1

bor-row the car __ keys. See you lat-er. Can I have them please?" _____ And the

Coda 1

Interlude

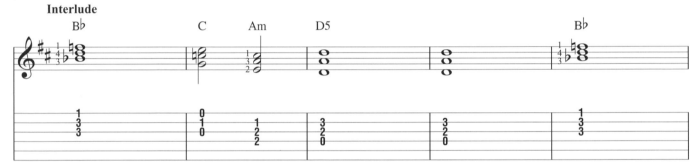

4. I've

Verse

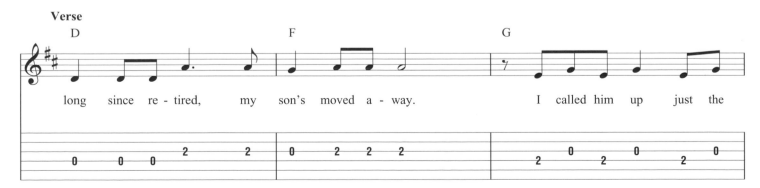

long since re-tired, my son's moved a-way. I called him up just the

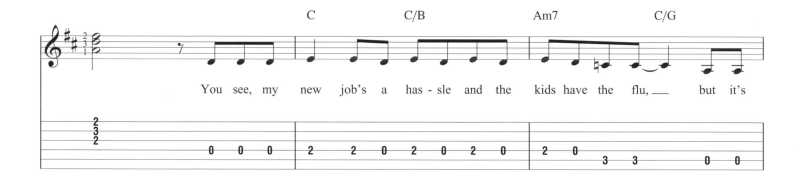

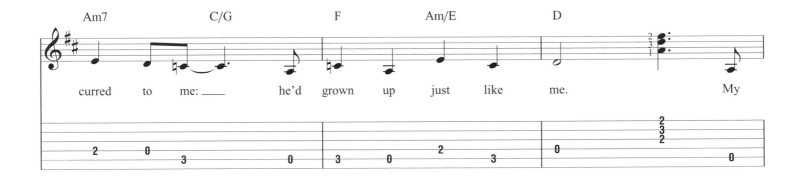

curred   to   me: ___   he'd   grown   up   just   like   me.   My

D.S. al Coda 2

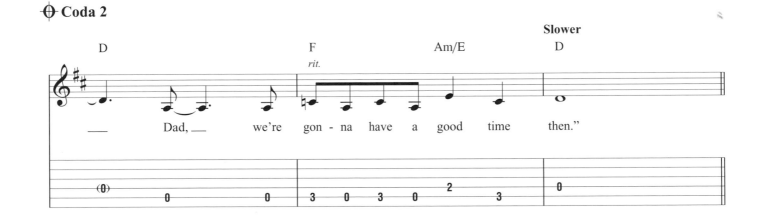

boy   was   just   like   me.   And   the

⊕ Coda 2

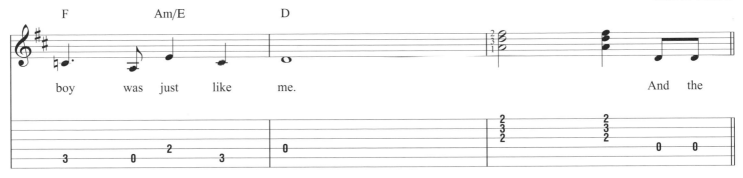

___   Dad, ___   we're   gon - na   have   a   good   time   then."

Outro

Additional Lyrics

2. My son turned ten just the other day;
   He said, "Thanks for the ball, Dad. Come on, let's play.
   Can you teach me to throw?"
   I said, "Not today, I got a lot to do."
   He said, "That's okay." And he, he walked away,
   But his smile never dimmed, it said,
   "I'm gonna be like him, yeah.
   You know I'm gonna be like him."

Catch the Wind

Words and Music by Donovan Leitch

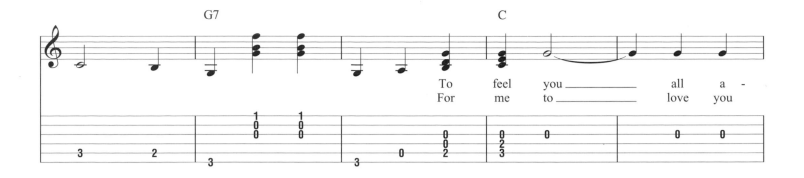

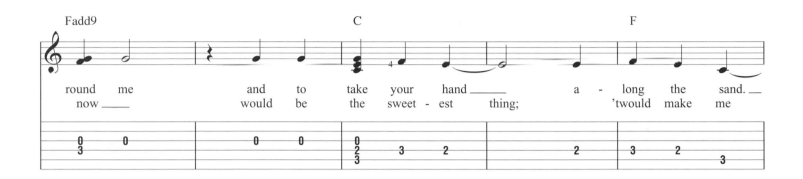

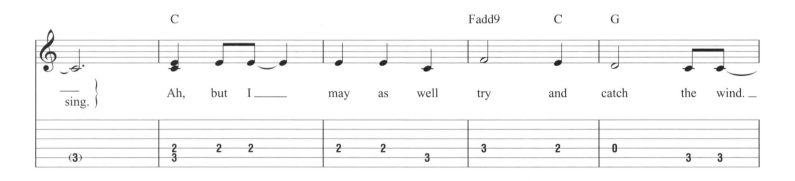

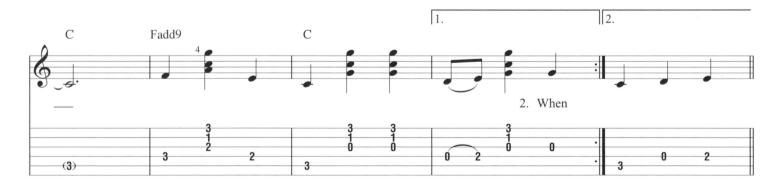

Interlude

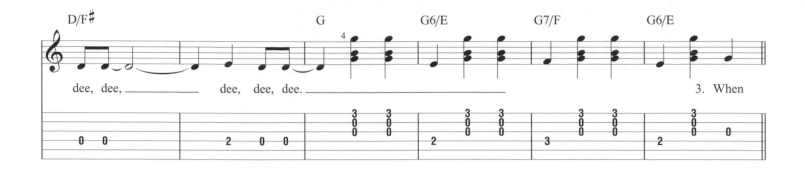

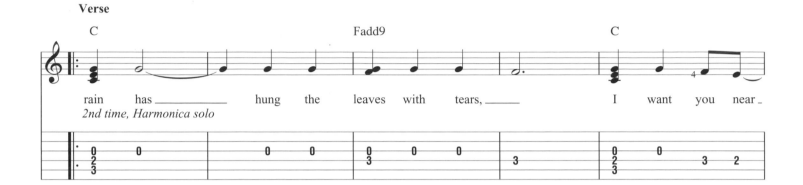

Verse

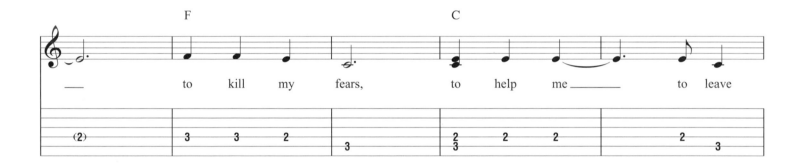

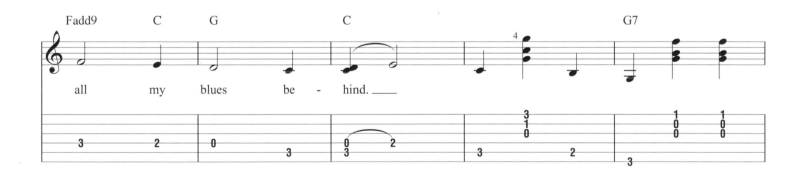

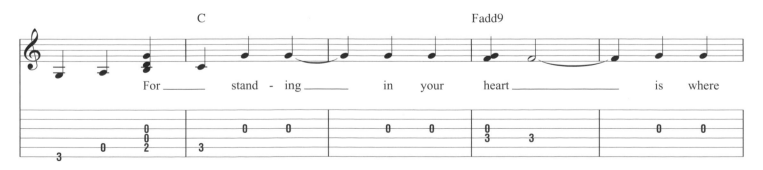

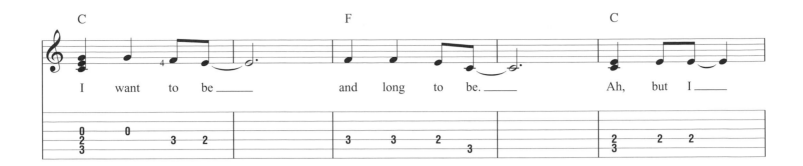

I want to be _____ and long to be. _____ Ah, but I _____

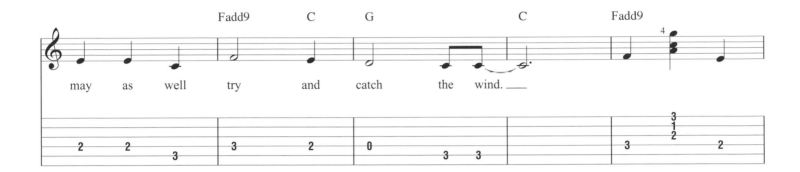

may as well try and catch the wind. _____

Outro

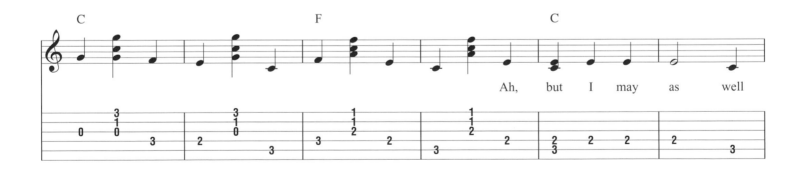

Harmonica solo ends

Ah, but I may as well

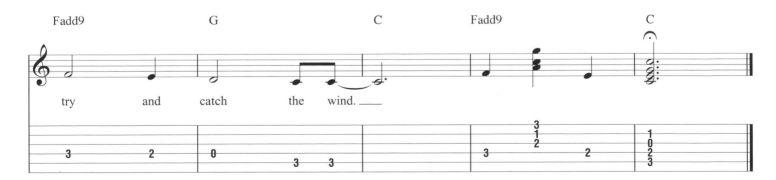

try and catch the wind. _____

Daydream Believer

Words and Music by John Stewart

shav-ing ra - zor's cold___ and it___ stings.

% Chorus

Cheer up sleep - y Jean._____ Oh, what can it mean to a

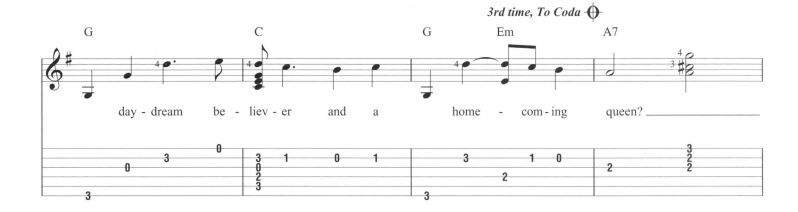

3rd time, To Coda ⊕

day - dream be - liev - er and a home - com - ing queen?_____

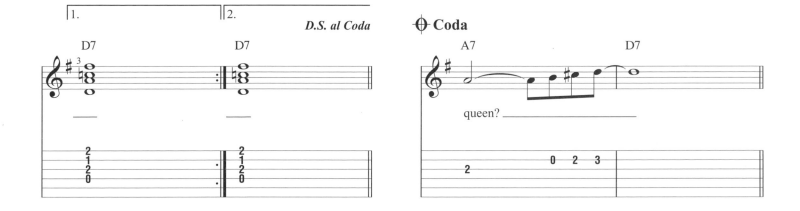

1. 2.

D.S. al Coda

⊕ **Coda**

queen?_____

Interlude

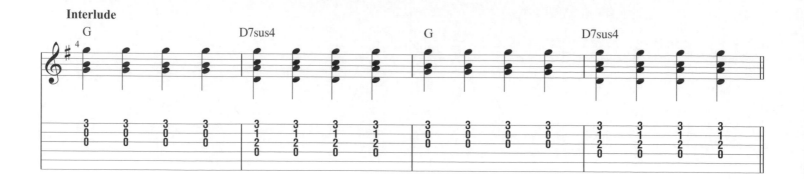

Outro-Chorus

Cheer up sleep - y Jean. _____ Oh, what can it

mean to a day - dream be - liev - er and a

Repeat and fade

home - com - ing queen? _____

Additional Lyrics

2. You once thought of me as a white knight on his steed.
   Now you know how happy I can be.
   Oh, and our good times start and end without dollar one to spend,
   But how much, baby, do we really need?

Doctor, My Eyes

Words and Music by Jackson Browne

Strum Pattern: 3
Pick Pattern: 3

done all that I could ___ to see the e - vil and the good ___ with-out hid -
go just where they will. ___ I nev - er no - ticed them un - til ___ I got this feel-

- ing. You must help me if you can. ___ Doc - tor, ___ my eyes. ___
- ing that it's lat - er than it seems. ___ Doc - tor, ___ my eyes. ___

Chorus

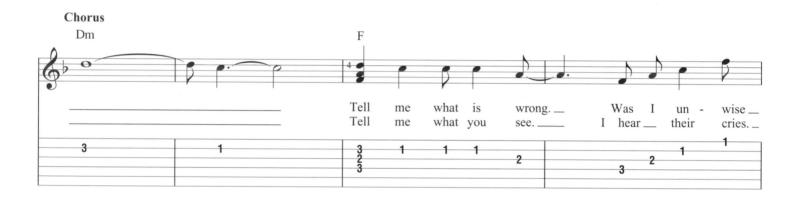

Tell me what is wrong. ___ Was I un - wise ___
Tell me what you see. ___ I hear ___ their cries. ___

Interlude

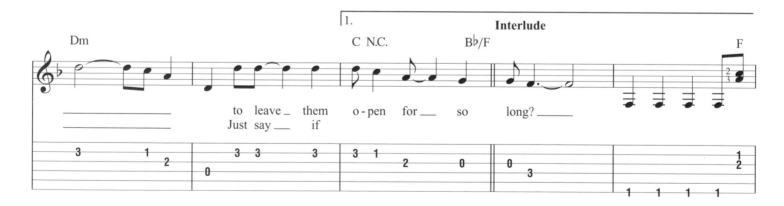

to leave ___ them o - pen for ___ so long? ___
Just say ___ if

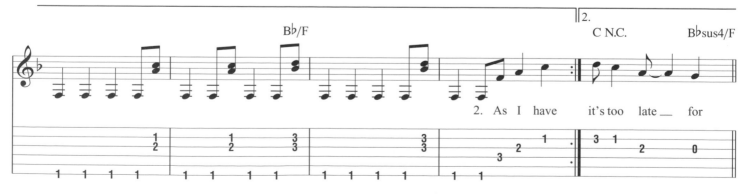

2. As I have it's too late ___ for

Interlude

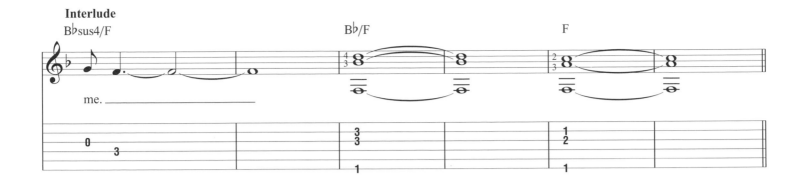

Guitar Solo

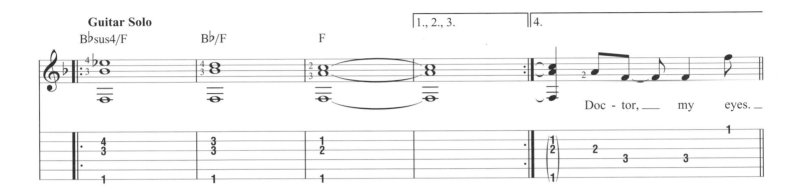

Chorus

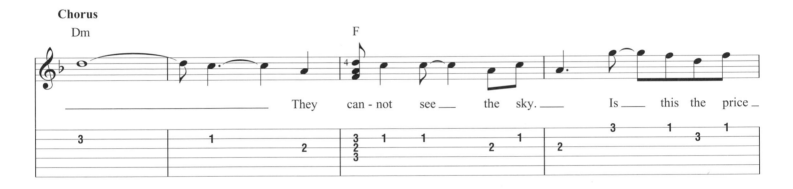

Outro

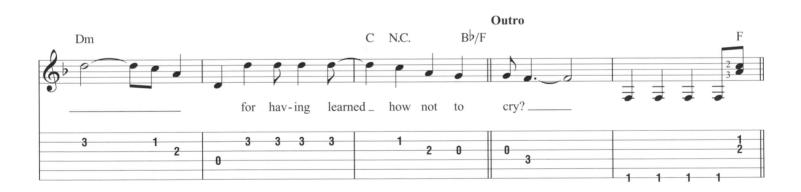

Repeat and fade

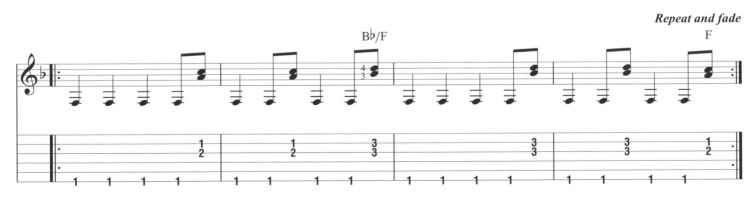

Dust in the Wind

Words and Music by Kerry Livgren

Strum Pattern: 3
Pick Pattern: 2

Intro
Moderately

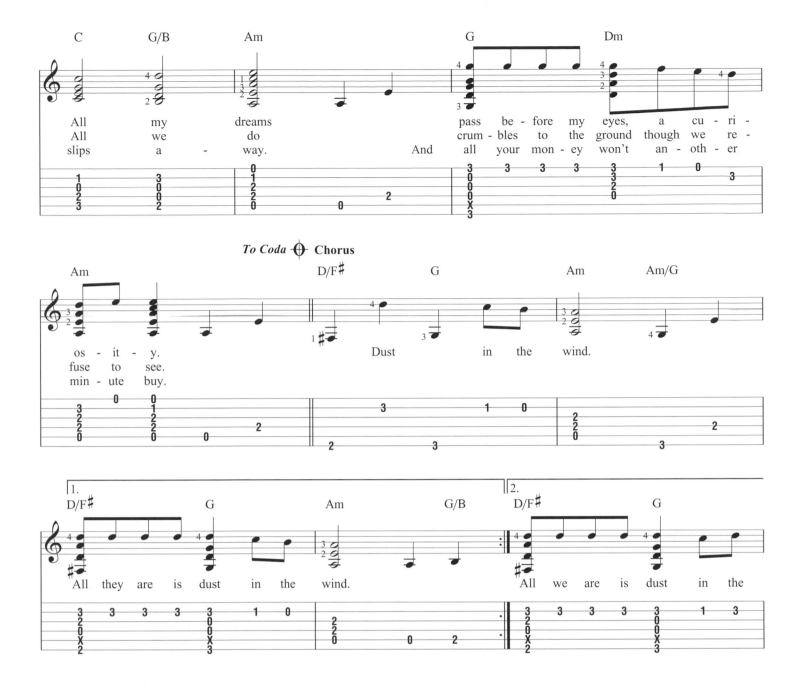

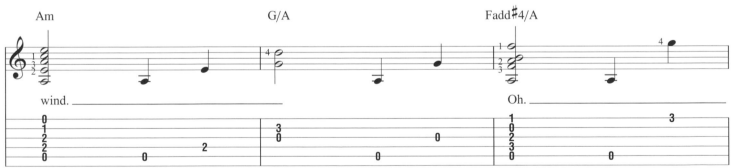

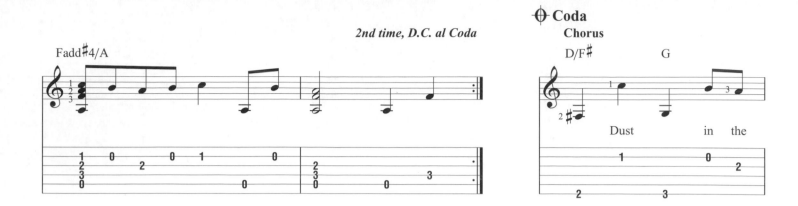

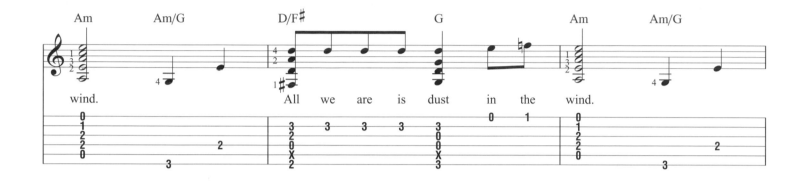

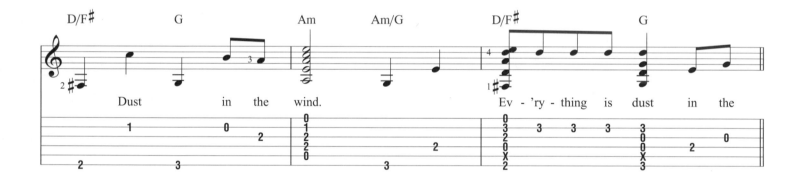

Follow the Drinkin' Gourd

Words and Music by Ronnie Gilbert, Lee Hays, Fred Hellerman and Pete Seeger

*Optional: To match recording, place capo at 1st fret.

**Sung one octave higher.

Verse

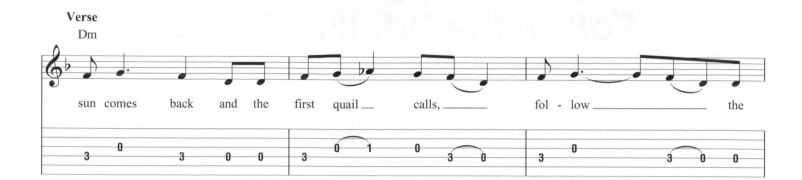

sun comes back and the first quail ___ calls, _____ fol - low _____ the

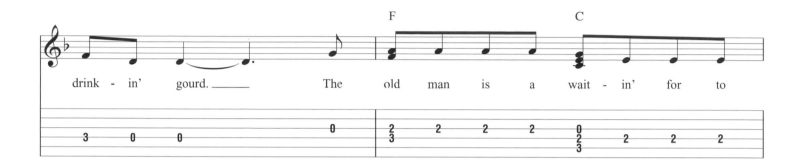

drink - in' gourd. _____ The old man is a wait - in' for to

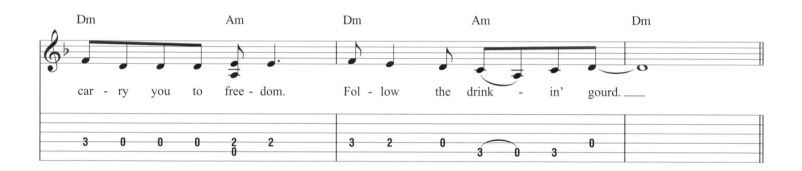

car - ry you to free - dom. Fol - low the drink - in' gourd. ___

𝄋 Chorus

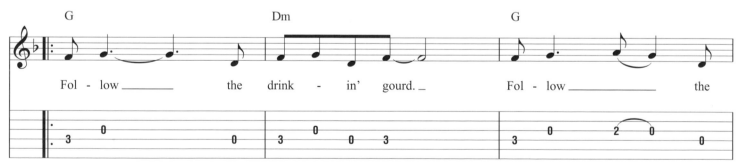

Fol - low _____ the drink - in' gourd. _ Fol - low _____ the

3rd time, To Coda ⊕

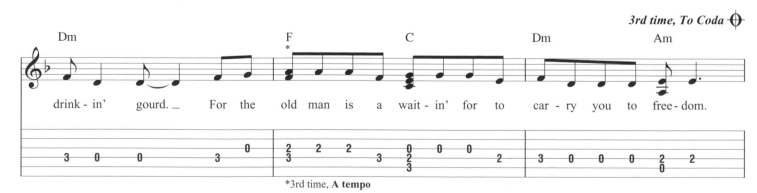

drink - in' gourd. _ For the old man is a wait - in' for to car - ry you to free - dom.

*3rd time, **A tempo**

44

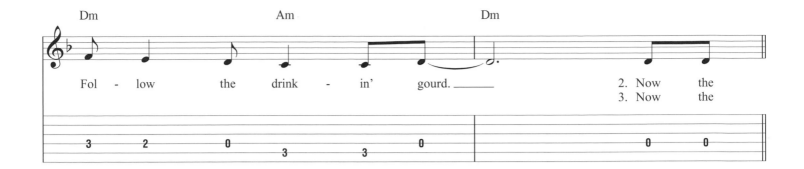

Verse
Faster

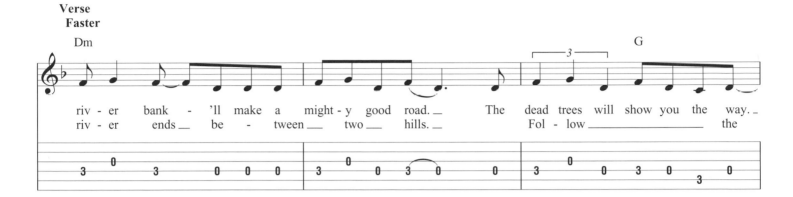

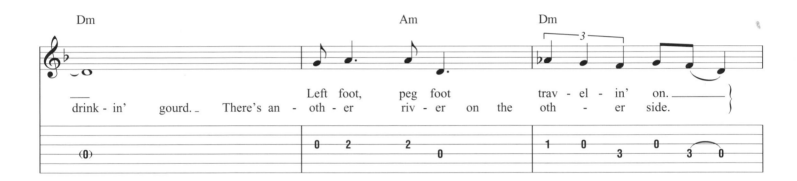

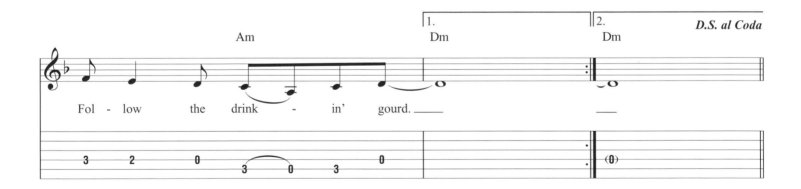

Coda

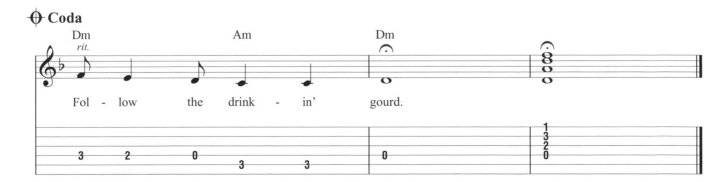

Everybody's Talkin'
(Echoes)

Words and Music by Fred Neil

Strum Pattern: 2, 4
Pick Pattern: 2, 3

Verse
Moderately

1., 3. Ev-'ry-bod-y's   talk-in' at me,   I don't hear a word they're say - in,'
2. *See additional lyrics*

_____ on - ly the ech - oes _____ of my mind. _____

Chorus

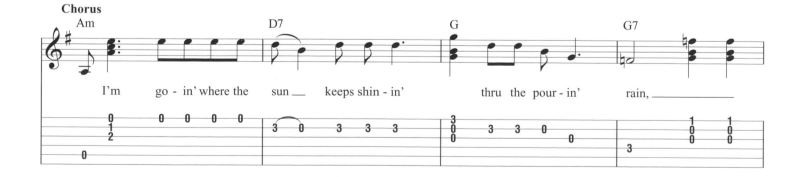

I'm go - in' where the sun _____ keeps shin - in' thru the pour - in' rain, _____

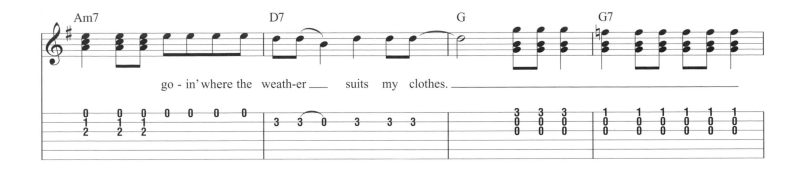

go - in' where the weath-er ___ suits my clothes. ___

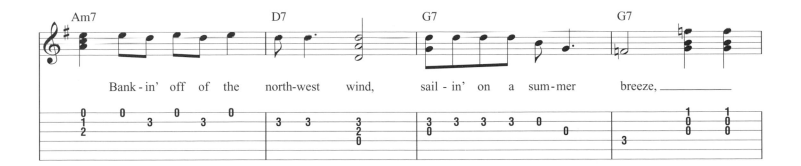

Bank - in' off of the north-west wind, sail - in' on a sum-mer breeze, ___

D.C. al Coda

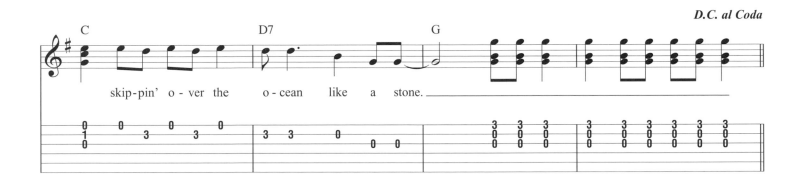

skip - pin' o - ver the o - cean like a stone. ___

⊕ **Coda**

Outro

_____ And I won't let you leave my love _ be-hind. _____ And

Additional Lyrics

2. People stoppin', starin',
   I can't see the faces,
   Only the shadows of their eyes.

Fire and Rain

Words and Music by James Taylor

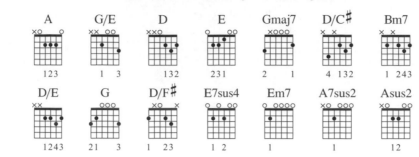

A   G/E   D   E   Gmaj7   D/C#   Bm7

D/E   G   D/F#   E7sus4   Em7   A7sus2   Asus2

Strum Pattern: 3
Pick Pattern: 3

Intro
Moderately, in 2

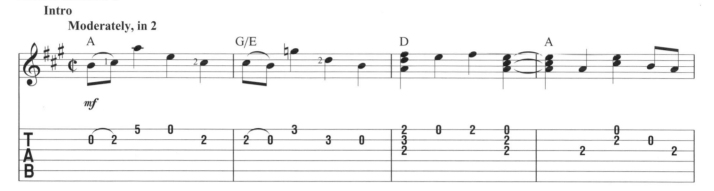

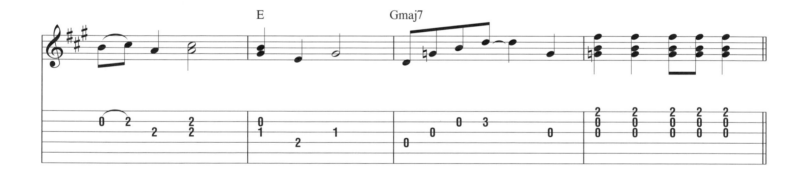

% Verse

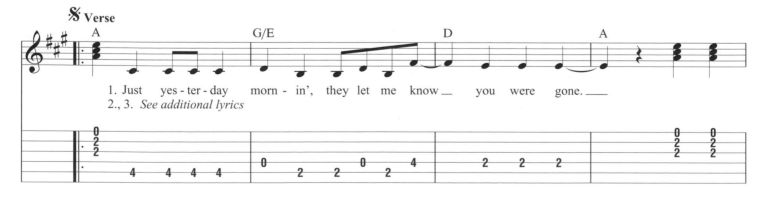

1. Just yes-ter-day morn-in', they let me know __ you were gone. __
2., 3. *See additional lyrics*

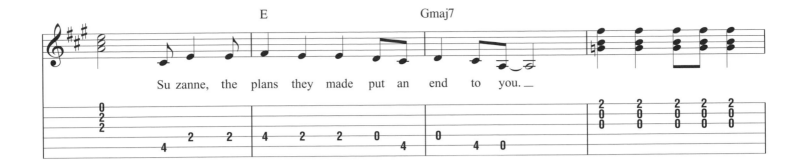

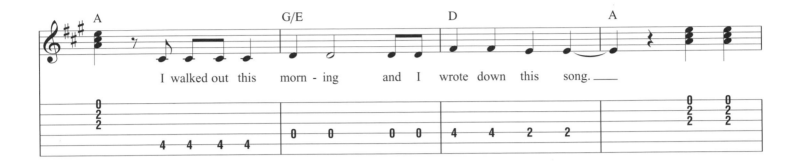

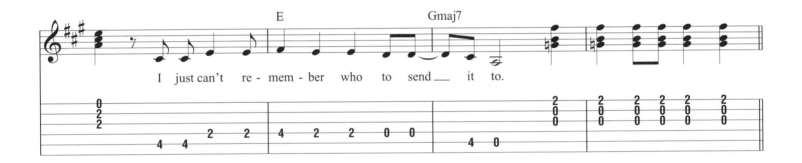

Chorus

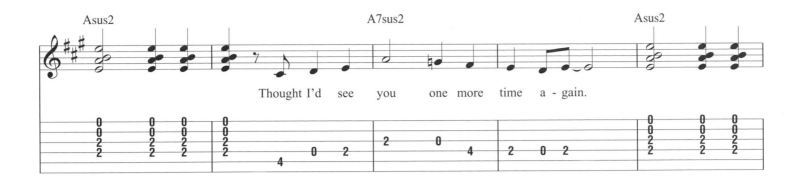

Thought I'd see you one more time a - gain.

There's just a few things com-ing my way this time a - round now.

Thought I'd see you, thought I'd see you, fire and rain now.

Outro
w/ Voc. ad lib.

Repeat and fade

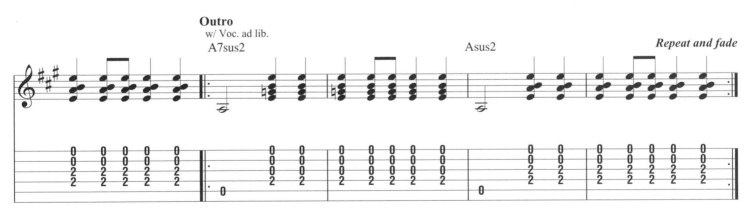

Additional Lyrics

2. Won't you look down upon me, Jesus, You got to help me make a stand.
   You've just got to see me through another day.
   My body's aching and my time is at hand.
   I won't make it any other way.

3. Been walking my mind to an easy time, my back turned towards the sun.
   Lord knows when the cold wind blows, it'll turn your head around.
   Well, there's hours of time on the telephone line to talk about things to come,
   Sweet dreams and flying machines in pieces on the ground.

For What It's Worth

Words and Music by Stephen Stills

Strum Pattern: 2
Pick Pattern: 4

Intro
Slow Rock

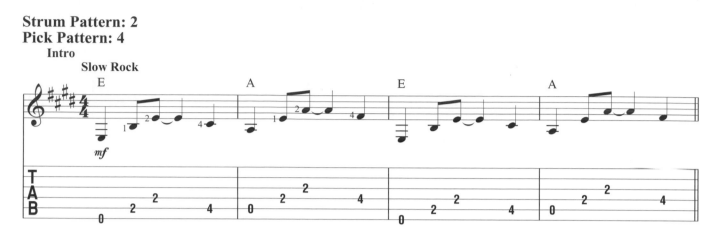

Verse

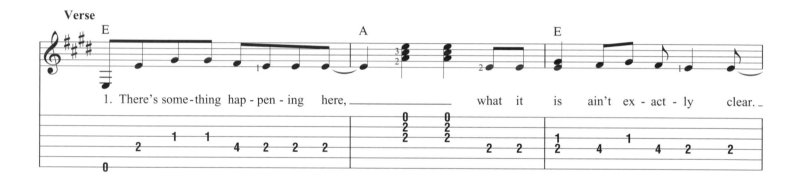

1. There's some-thing hap-pen-ing here, _____ what it is ain't ex-act-ly clear. _____

_____ There's a man with a gun o-ver there, _____ tell-in'

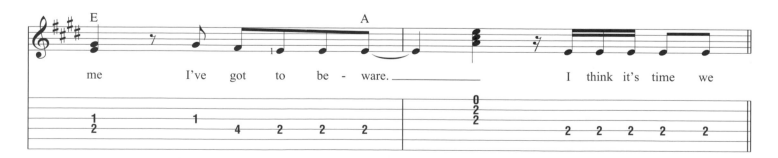

me I've got to be-ware. _____ I think it's time we

Chorus

stop, chil - dren, what's that sound? __ Ev - 'ry - bod - y look what's go - in' down. _____

Verse

2. There's bat - tle lines be - in' drawn, _____ no - bod - y's right if ev - 'ry - bod - y's
3., 4. *See additional lyrics*

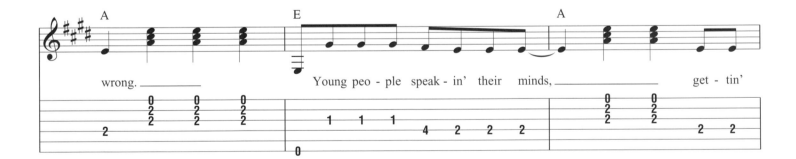

wrong. _____ Young peo - ple speak - in' their minds, _____ get - tin'

To Coda ⊕   **Chorus**

so much re - sist - ance from be - hind. I think it's time we stop, chil - dren, what's that sound?

Ev-'ry-bod-y look what's go-in' down. _____

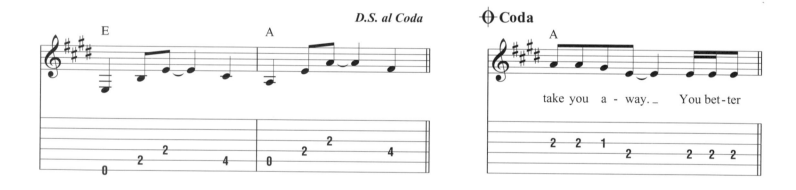

D.S. al Coda   ✛ **Coda**

take you a - way. _   You bet-ter

Outro-Chorus   *Repeat and fade*

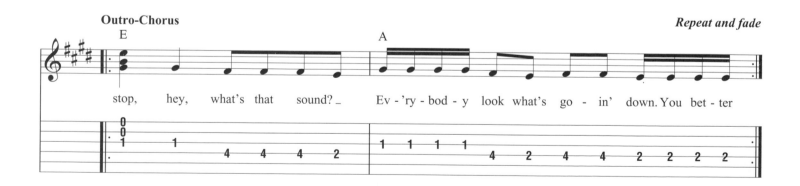

stop,   hey,   what's that   sound? _   Ev-'ry-bod-y look what's go-in' down. You bet-ter

Additional Lyrics

3. What a field day for the heat.
   A thousand people in the street
   Singin' songs and carryin' signs,
   Mostly saying, "Hooray for our side."

4. Paranoia strikes deep,
   Into your life it will creep.
   It starts when you're always afraid.
   Step out of line, the men come and take you away.

Goodnight, Irene

Words and Music by Huddie Ledbetter and John A. Lomax

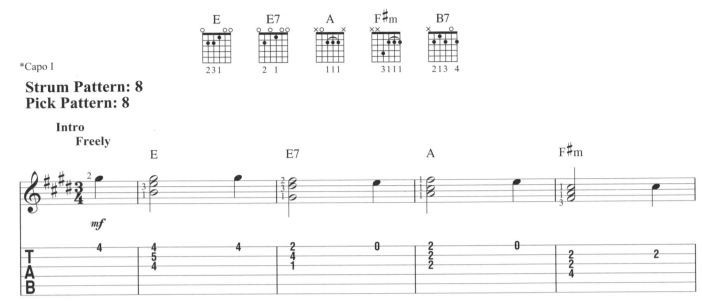

*Capo I

Strum Pattern: 8
Pick Pattern: 8

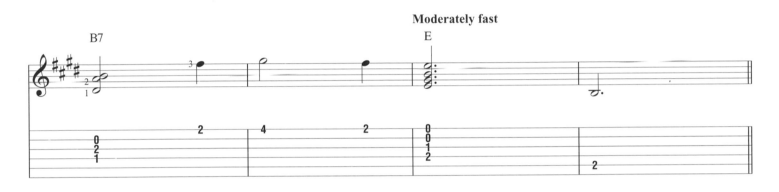

*Optional: To match recording, place capo at 1st fret.

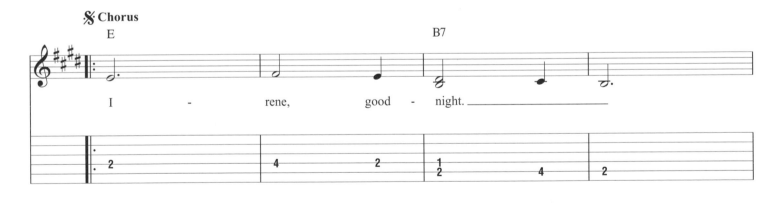

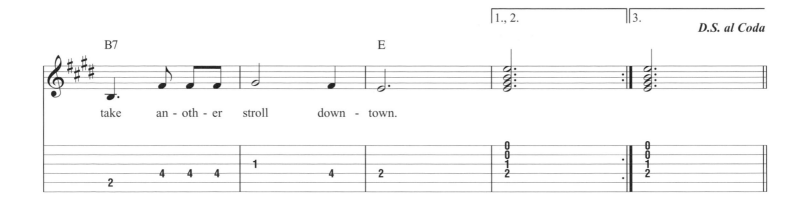

take an - oth - er stroll down - town.

Coda

Outro

Good - night, I - rene, good - night, I -

rene, I'll see you in my dreams. Good -

Additional Lyrics

2. Sometimes I live in the country,
Sometimes I live in town.
Sometimes I take a great notion
To jump into the river and drown.

3. Stop ramblin', stop your gamblin',
Stop stayin' out late at night.
Go home to your wife and fam'ly,
Stay there by your fireside bright.

Guantanamera

Musical Adaptation by Pete Seeger and Julian Orbon
Lyric Adaptation by Julian Orbon, based on a poem by Jose Marti
Lyric Editor: Hector Angulo
Original Music and Lyrics by Jose Fernandez Diaz

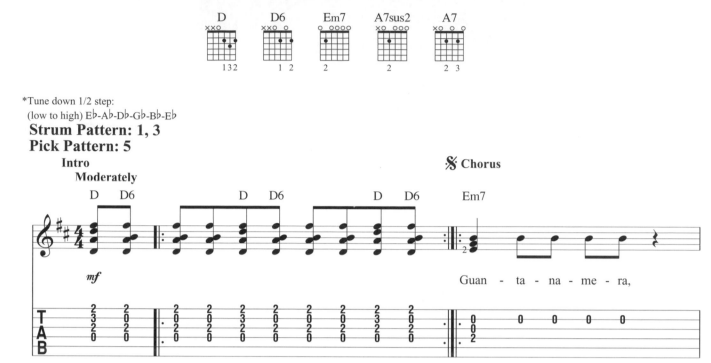

*Tune down 1/2 step:
(low to high) E♭-A♭-D♭-G♭-B♭-E♭

Strum Pattern: 1, 3
Pick Pattern: 5

* Optional: To match recording, tune down 1/2 step.

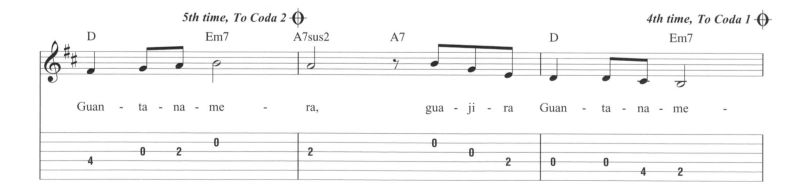

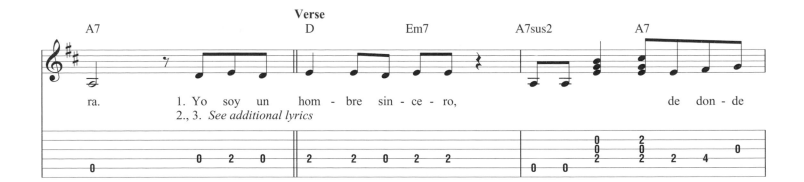

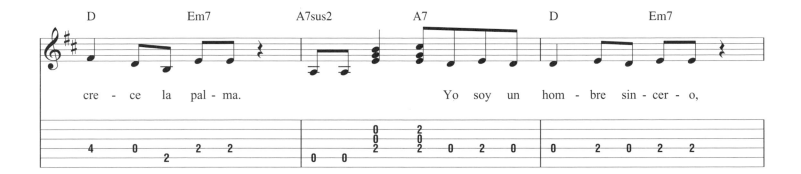

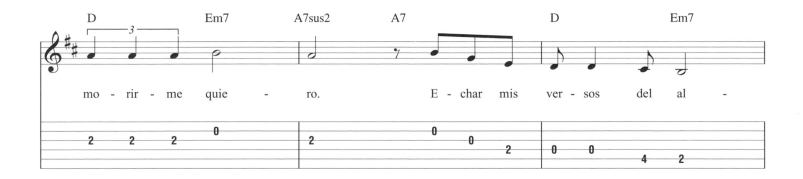

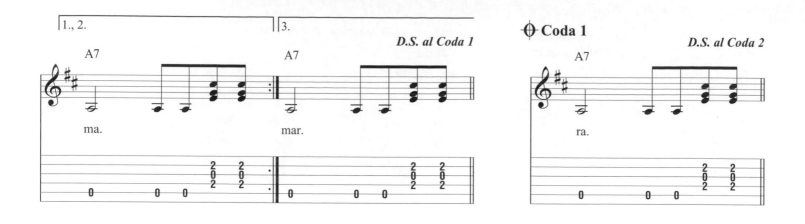

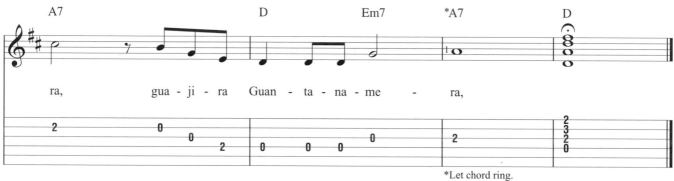

*Let chord ring.

Additional Lyrics

2. Mi verso es de un verde claro
   Y de un carmin encendido
   Mi verso es de un verde claro
   Y de un carmin encendido
   Mi verso es un cierro herido
   Que busca en el monte amparo.

3. Con los pobres de la tierra
   Quiero you mi suerte echar
   Con los pobres de la tierra
   Quiero yo mi suerte echar
   El arroyo do la sierra
   Me complace mas que el mar.

(Literal English Translation)

1. I am a truthful man, from the
   land of palm trees. Before
   dying, I want to share these
   poems of my soul.

2. My poems are light green,
   but they are also flaming
   crimson. My verses are like
   a wounded fawn, seeking
   refuge in the forest.

3. With the poor people of this
   earth, I want to share my fate.
   The little streams of the
   mountains please me more
   than the sea.

Hallelujah

Words and Music by Leonard Cohen

*Capo V

Strum Pattern: 8
Pick Pattern: 8

*Optional: To match recording, place capo at 5th fret.

heard there was a se-cret chord ___ that Da-vid played ___ and it

2. - 5. See additional lyrics

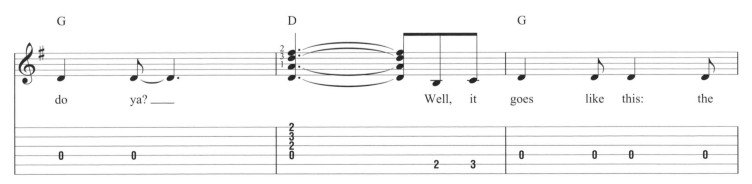

pleased the Lord. But you don't ___ real-ly care for mu - sic,

do ya? ___ Well, it goes like this: the

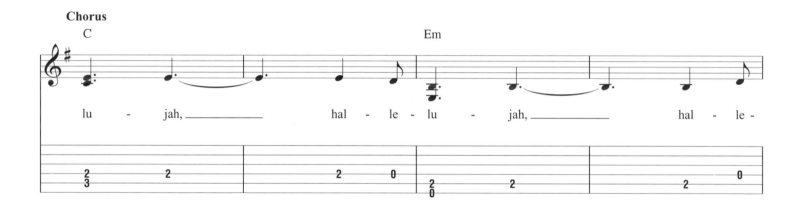

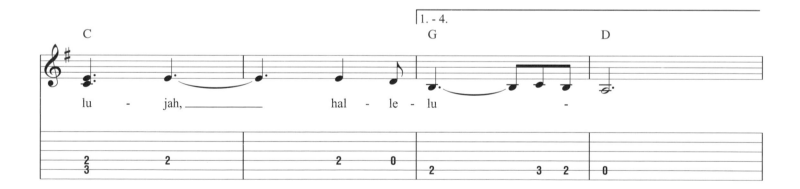

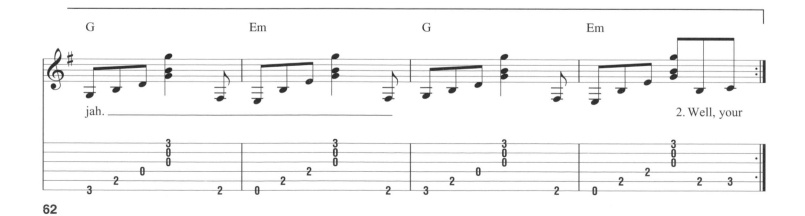

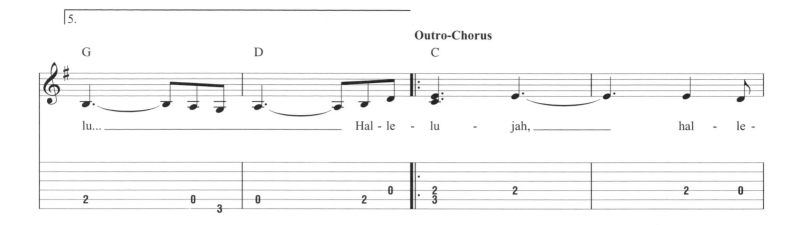

Additional Lyrics

2. Well, your faith was strong, but you needed proof.
   You saw her bathing on the roof.
   Her beauty and the moonlight overthrew ya.
   She tied you to her kitchen chair,
   And she broke your throne and she cut your hair,
   And from your lips she drew the hallelujah.

3. Well, baby, I've been here before,
   I've seen this room and I've walked this floor,
   You know, I used to live alone before I knew ya.
   And I've seen your flag on the marble arch,
   And love is not a vict'ry march,
   It's a cold and it's a broken hallelujah.

4. Well, there was a time when you let me know
   What's really going on below.
   But now you never show that to me, do ya?
   But remember when I moved in you
   And the holy dove was moving too,
   And ev'ry breath we drew was hallelujah.

5. Maybe there is a God above,
   But all I've ever learned from love
   Was how to shoot somebody who outdrew ya.
   And it's not a cry that you hear at night,
   It's not somebody who's seen the light,
   It's a cold and it's a broken hallelujah.

Guinnevere

Words and Music by David Crosby

*Strum Pattern: 2
*Pick Pattern: 2

*Use Pattern 9 for ¾ meas.

**Gtr. in Open Em11 tuning arr. for standard tuning.

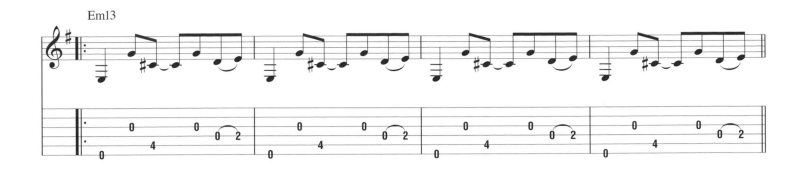

𝄋 Verse

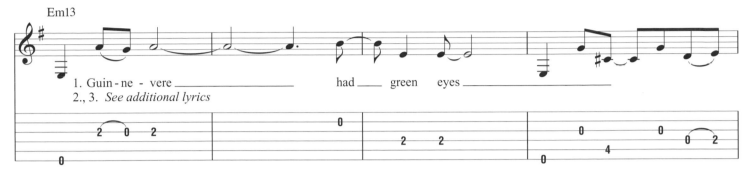

1. Guin - ne - vere _____ had _____ green eyes _____
2., 3. *See additional lyrics*

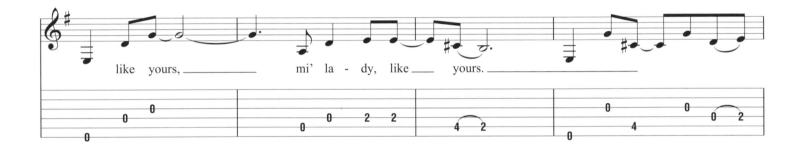

like yours, _____ mi' la - dy, like _____ yours. _____

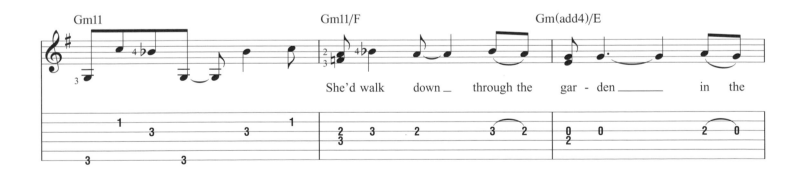

She'd walk down _____ through the gar - den _____ in the

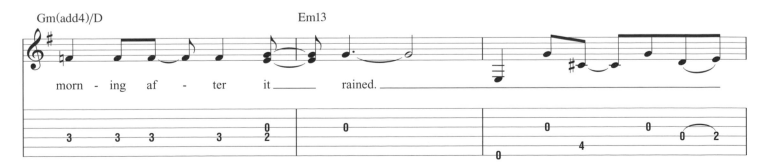

morn - ing af - ter it _____ rained. _____

Gsus4

Pea-cocks wan - dered

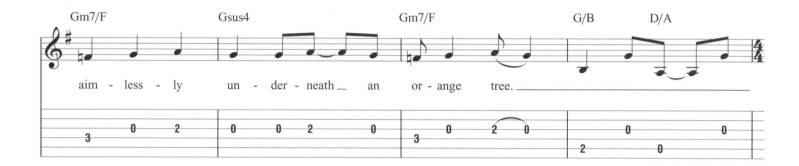

Gm7/F   Gsus4   Gm7/F   G/B   D/A

aim - less - ly   un - der - neath   an   or - ange   tree. ___

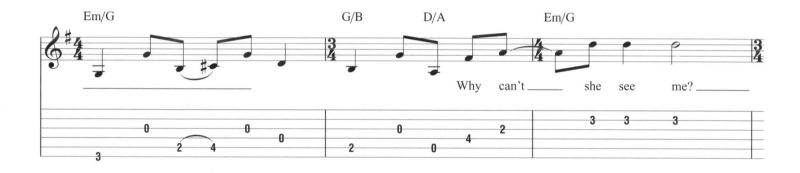

Em/G   G/B   D/A   Em/G

Why   can't ___   she   see   me? ___

3rd time, To Coda 1 ⊕

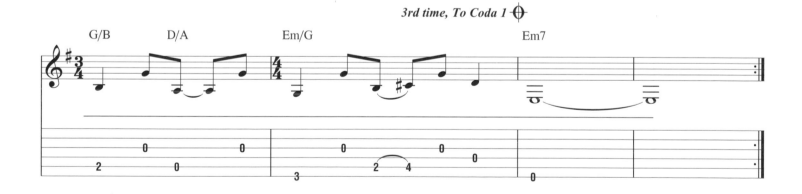

G/B   D/A   Em/G   Em7

Bridge

Bm9

66

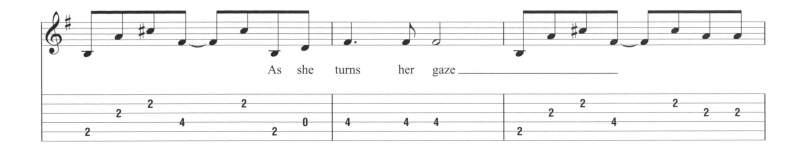

As she turns her gaze _____

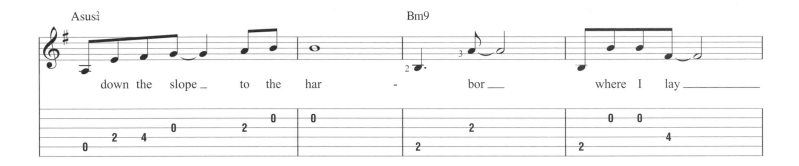

Asus²₄   Bm9

down the slope _ to the har   -   bor __   where I lay _____

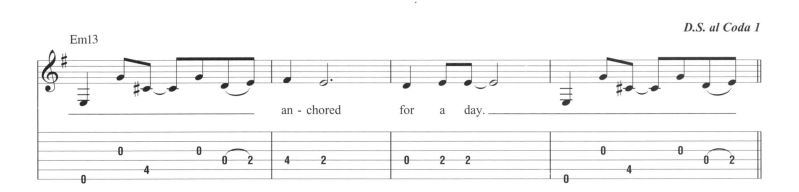

D.S. al Coda 1

Em13

an - chored   for   a   day. _____

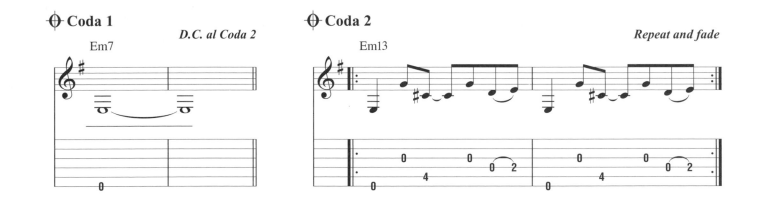

⊕ **Coda 1**

D.C. al Coda 2

Em7

⊕ **Coda 2**

Repeat and fade

Em13

Additional Lyrics

2. Guinnevere drew pentagrams like yours, mi' lady, like yours.
   Late at night, when she thought that no one was watching at all, on the wall.
   (Do, do, do, do, do, do, do. Do, do, do, do, do, do, do.)
   She shall be free.

3. Guinnevere had golden hair like yours, mi' lady, like yours.
   Streaming out when we'd ride through the warm wind down by the bay yesterday.
   Seagulls circle endlessly, I sing in silent harmony.
   We shall be free.

A Horse with No Name

Words and Music by Dewey Bunnell

Em D$^6_9$/F#

Strum Pattern: 1
Pick Pattern: 3

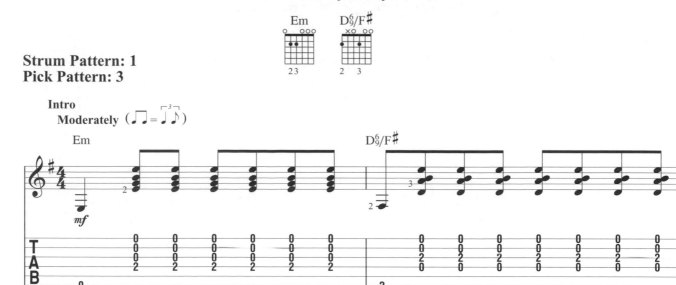

Intro
Moderately

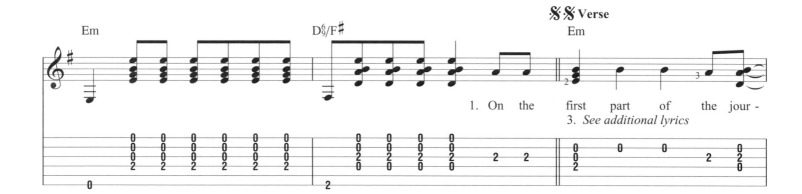

Verse

1. On the first part of the jour-
3. *See additional lyrics*

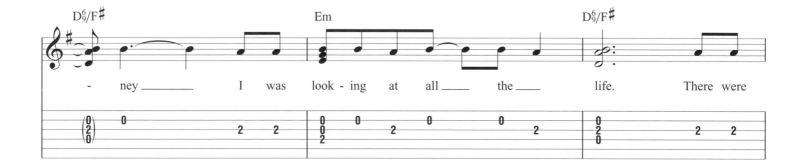

-ney ____ I was look-ing at all ____ the ____ life. There were

plants and birds ___ and rocks and things. ___ There was sand and hills ___ and

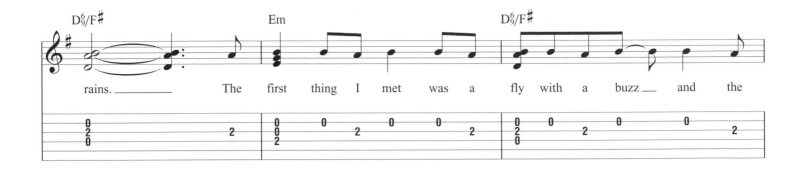

rains. _____ The first thing I met was a fly with a buzz ____ and the

sky with no ____ clouds. _____ The heat was hot ____ and the

ground was dry, ___ but the air was full ____ of ____ sounds. _____ I've

𝄋 Chorus

been through the des-ert on a horse with no name. _ It felt good to be out ___ of the

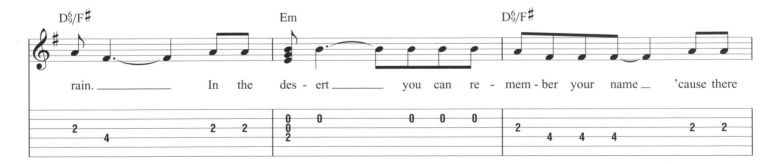

rain. _____ In the des-ert _____ you can re-mem-ber your name _ 'cause there

2nd time, To Coda 1 ⊕

3rd time, To Coda 2 ⊕

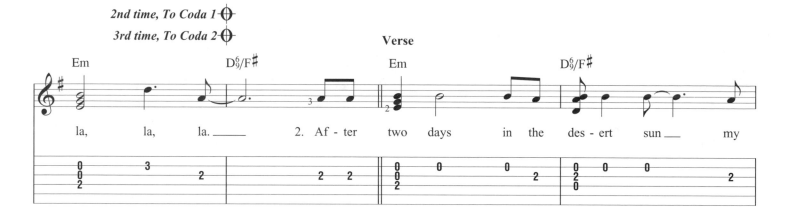

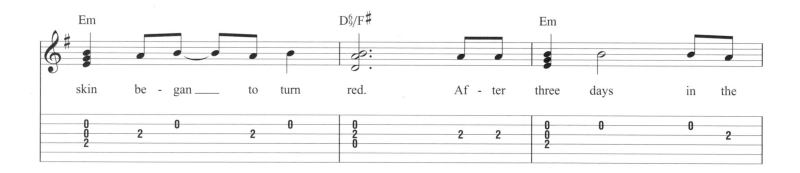

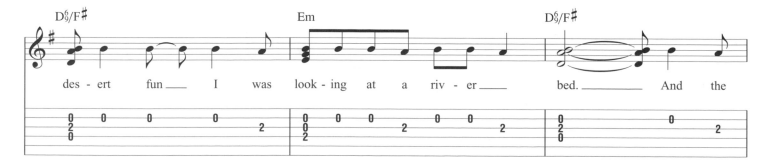

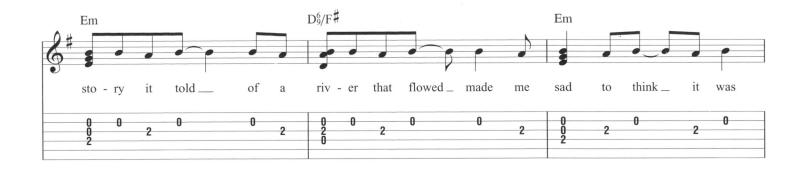

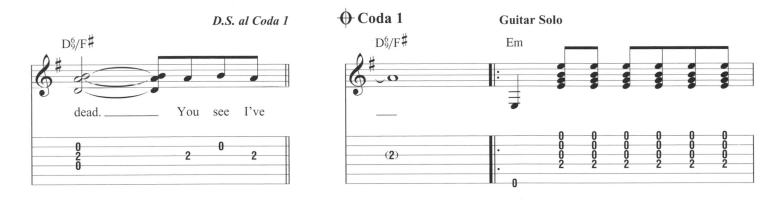

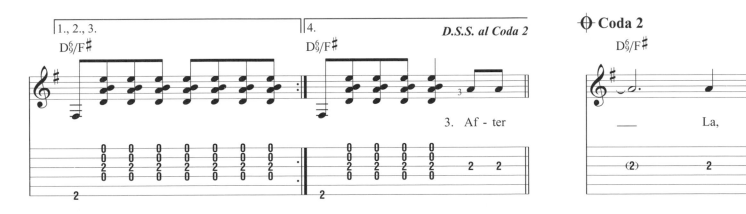

Additional Lyrics

3. After nine days I let the horse run free
   'Cause the desert had turned to sea.
   There were plants and birds and rocks and things.
   There was sand and hills and rains.
   The ocean is a desert with its life underground
   And the perfect disguise above.
   Under the cities lies a heart made of ground,
   But the humans will give no love.
   You see I've…

If I Had a Hammer
(The Hammer Song)

Words and Music by Lee Hays and Pete Seeger

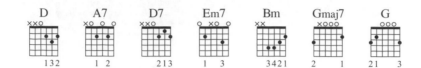

Strum Pattern: 2, 3
Pick Pattern: 2, 3

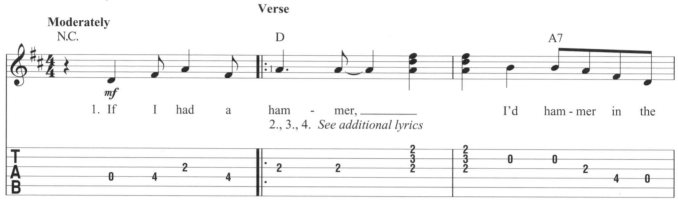

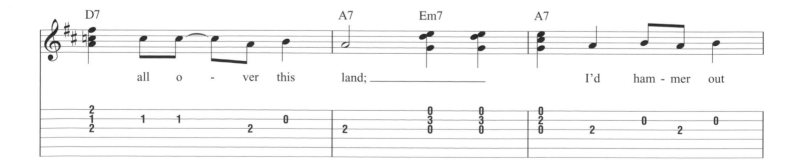

dan - ger, _____ I'd ham - mer out a warn - ing, _____

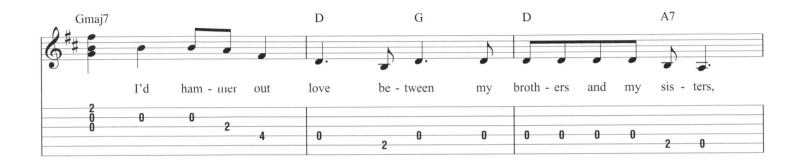

I'd ham - mer out love be - tween my broth - ers and my sis - ters,

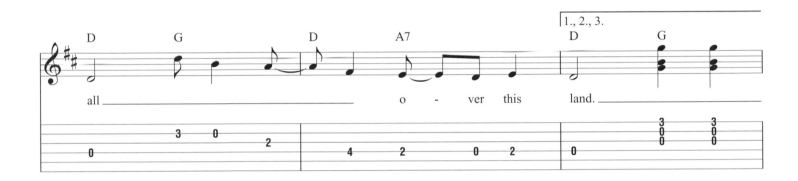

all _____ o - ver this land. _____

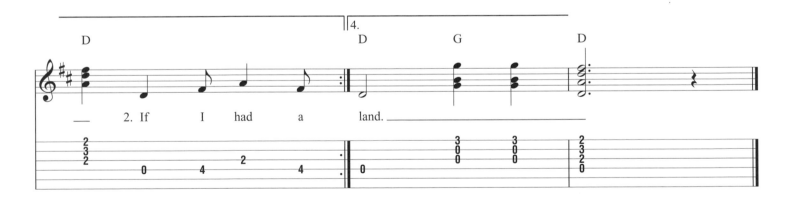

___ 2. If I had a land. _____

Additional Lyrics

2. If I had a bell, I'd ring it in the morning,
   I'd ring it in the ev'ning all over this land;
   I'd ring out danger, I'd ring out a warning,
   I'd ring out love between my brothers and my sisters,
   All over this land.

3. If I had a song, I'd sing it in the morning,
   I'd sing it in the ev'ning all over this land;
   I'd sing out danger, I'd sing out warning,
   I'd sing out love between my brothers and my sisters,
   All over this land.

4. Well, I got a hammer, and I've got a bell,
   And I've got a song to sing all over this land;
   It's the hammer of justice, it's the bell of freedom,
   It's the song about love between my brothers and my sisters,
   All over this land.

Last Night I Had the Strangest Dream

Words and Music by Ed McCurdy

C   F   G7   Am   Dm   C7

*Tune down 1/2 step:
(low to high) Eb-Ab-Db-Gb-Bb-Eb

Strum Pattern: 8, 9
Pick Pattern: 9

Intro
Moderately

§ Verse

C

*Optional: To match recording, tune down 1/2 step.

1. Last (3., 4.) night I had the
2. See additional lyrics

strang - est dream I'd ev - er dreamed __ be - fore.

4th time, To Coda ⊕

I dreamed the world had all a - greed to

put an end _____ to war. I dreamed I

Additional Lyrics

2. And when the paper was all signed and a million copies made,
They all joined hands and bowed their heads, and grateful prayers were prayed.
And the people in the streets below were dancing 'round and 'round.
And swords and guns and uniforms were scattered on the ground.

Mr. Tambourine Man

Words and Music by Bob Dylan

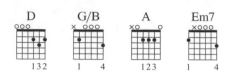

*Drop D tuning, capo III:

Strum Pattern: 1, 3
Pick Pattern: 3, 5

Intro
Moderately, in 2

*Optional: To match recording, place capo at 3rd fret.

Chorus

Hey! Mis - ter Tam - bou - rine Man, play a song for me. I'm not

sleep - y, and there is no place I'm go - ing to.

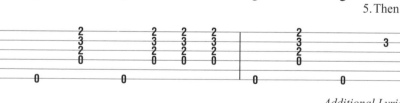

Additional Lyrics

2. Take me on a trip upon your magic swirlin' ship,
   My senses have been stripped, my hands can't feel to grip.
   My toes too numb to step, wait only for my boot heels
   To be wanderin'.
   I'm ready to go anywhere, I'm ready for to fade
   Into my own parade, cast your dancing spell my way,
   I promise to go under it.

5. Then take me disappearin' through the smoke rings of my mind,
   Down the foggy ruins of time, far past the frozen leaves,
   The haunted, frightened trees out to the windy beach,
   Far from the twisted reach of crazy sorrow.
   Yes, to dance beneath the diamond sky with one hand waving free,
   Silhouetted by the sea, circled by the circus sands,
   With all memory and fate driven deep beneath the waves.
   Let me forget about today until tomorrow.

3. Though you might hear laughin', spinnin', swingin' madly across the sun,
   It's not aimed at anyone, it's just escapin' on the run,
   And but for the sky there are no fences facin',
   And if you hear vague traces of skippin' reels of rhyme,
   To your tambourine in time, it's just a ragged clown behind,
   I wouldn't pay it any mind, it's just a shadow you're
   Seein' that he's chasing.

Puff the Magic Dragon

Words and Music by Lenny Lipton and Peter Yarrow

G   Bm   C   Em   A7   D7

*Capo II

Strum Pattern: 6
Pick Pattern: 6

Verse
Moderately fast

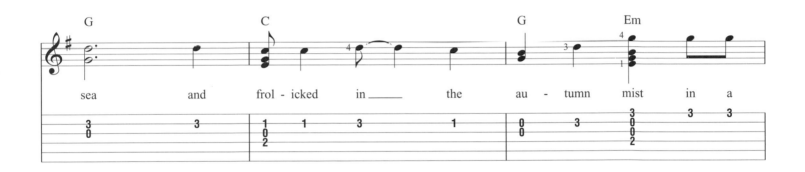

1. Puff, the mag-ic drag-on lived by the
2., 3., 4. *See additional lyrics*

*Optional: To match recording, place capo at 2nd fret.

sea and frol-icked in ____ the au-tumn mist in a

land called Hon-a-lee. Lit-tle Jack-ie

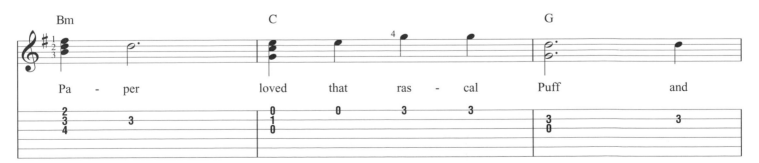

Pa-per loved that ras-cal Puff and

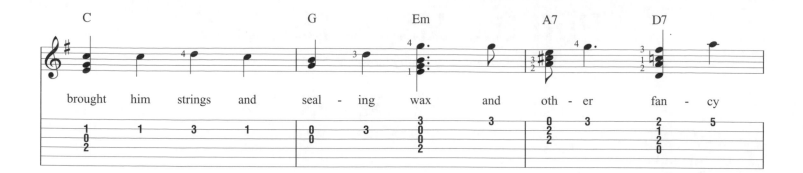

brought him strings and seal - ing wax and oth - er fan - cy

Chorus

stuff. Oh! Puff the mag - ic drag - on

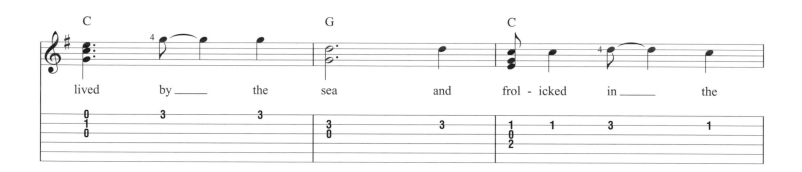

lived by ___ the sea and frol - icked in ___ the

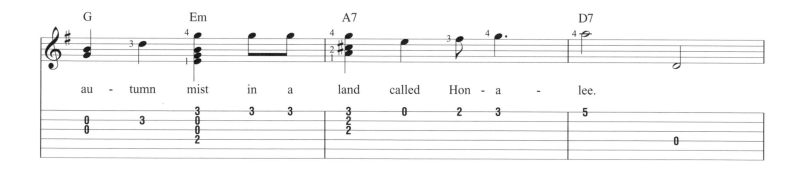

au - tumn mist in a land called Hon - a - lee.

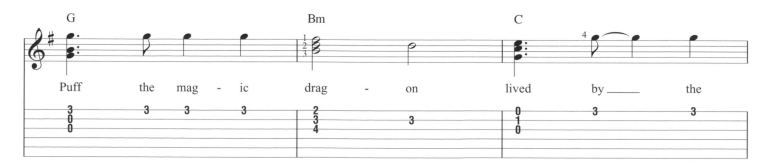

Puff the mag - ic drag - on lived by ___ the

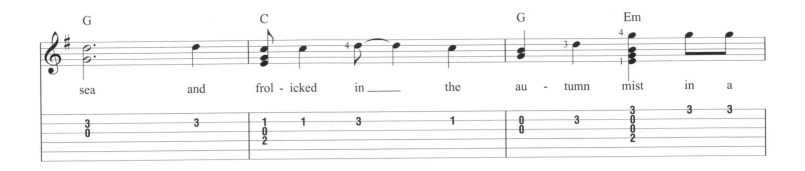

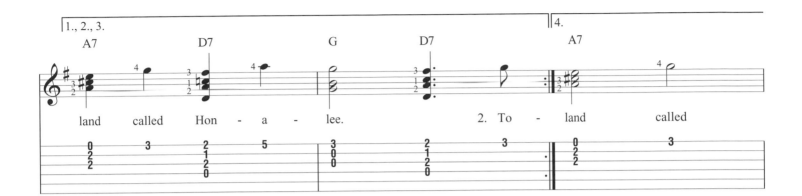

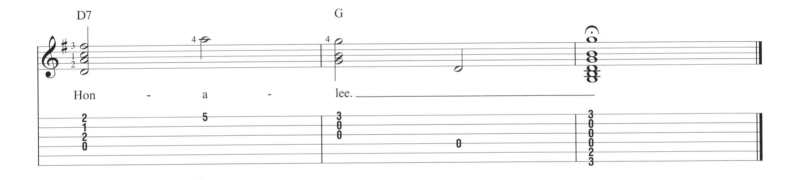

Additional Lyrics

2. Together they would travel on a boat with billowed sail.
   Jackie kept a lookout perched on Puff's gigantic tail.
   Noble kings and princes would bow when e'er they came.
   Pirate ships would low'r their flags when Puff roared out his name. Oh!

3. A dragon lives forever, but not so little boys.
   Painted wings and giant's rings make way for other toys.
   One gray night it happened, Jackie Paper came no more,
   And Puff that mighty dragon, he ceased his fearless roar.

4. His head was bent in sorrow, green scales fell like rain.
   Puff no longer went to play along the Cherry Lane.
   Without his lifelong friend, Puff could not be brave,
   So Puff that mighty dragon sadly slipped into his cave. Oh!

San Francisco Bay Blues

Words and Music by Jesse Fuller

Strum Pattern: 3
Pick Pattern: 3

*Sung one octave lower.

did-n't mean to treat her so bad.   She was the best gal I ev-er

had.   Well, __ she said good-bye, __ and she made __ me cry. __

Verse

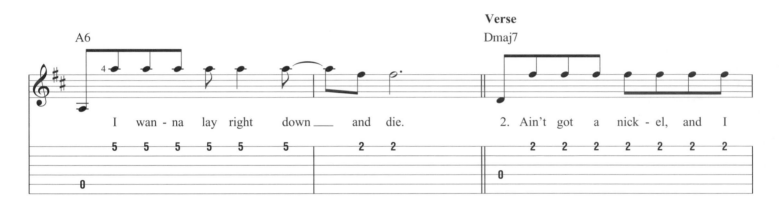

I wan-na lay right down __ and die.   2. Ain't got a nick-el, and I

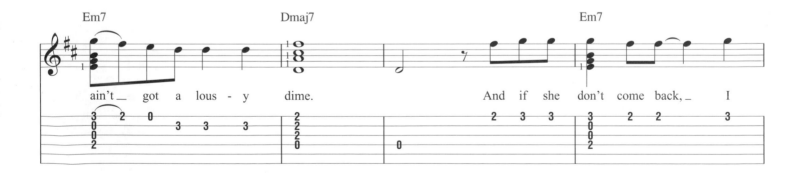

ain't __ got a lous-y dime.   And if she don't come back, __ I

guess I'm gon-na lose my mind.   If she ev-er comes back to

stay, gon-na be an-oth-er brand-new day _____ when I go

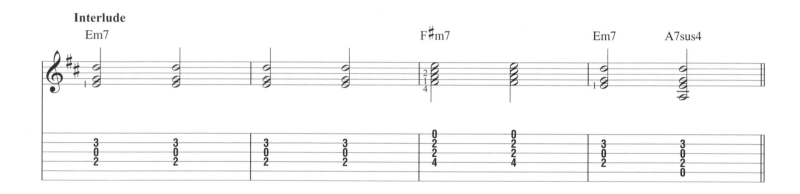

walk-in' with my ba-by down by the San Fran-cis-co Bay. ___

Interlude

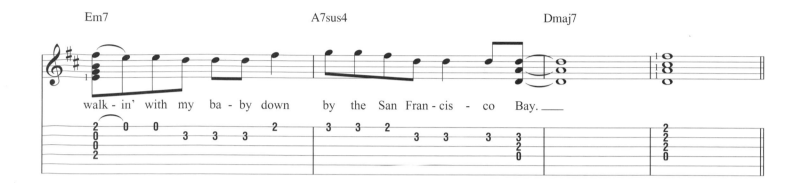

Verse

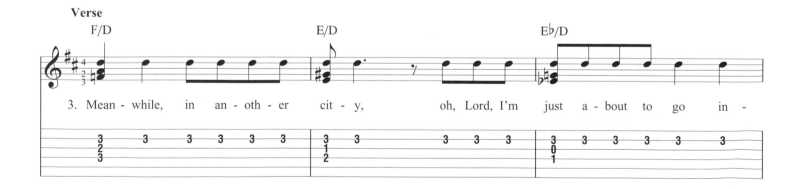

3. Mean-while, in an-oth-er cit-y, oh, Lord, I'm just a-bout to go in-

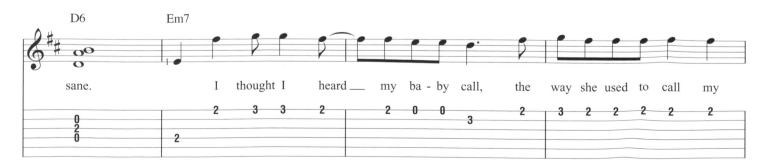

sane. I thought I heard ___ my ba-by call, the way she used to call my

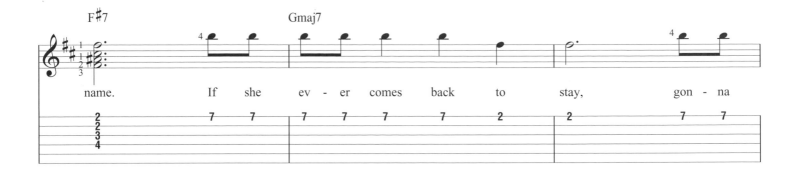

name. If she ev-er comes back to stay, gon-na

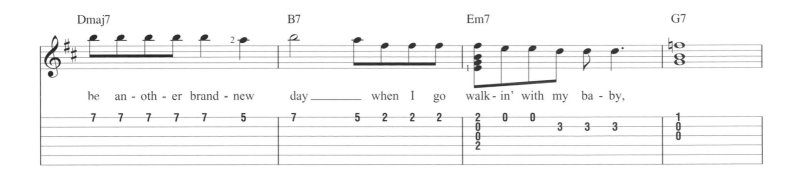

be an-oth-er brand-new day _____ when I go walk-in' with my ba-by,

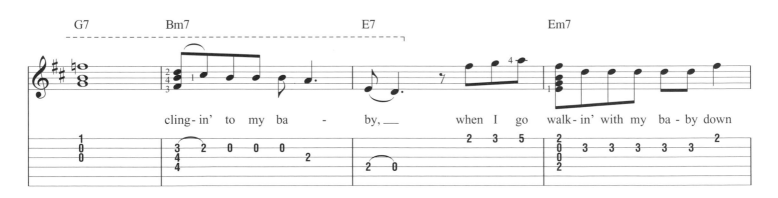

talk-in' to my ba-by, sing - in' to my ba-by,

*Sung as written.

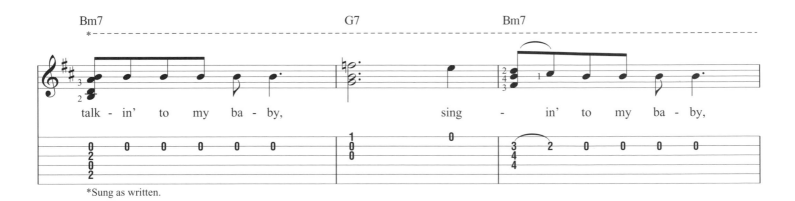

cling-in' to my ba - by, ___ when I go walk-in' with my ba-by down

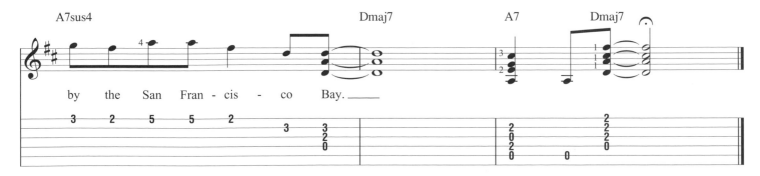

by the San Fran-cis - co Bay. _____

Scotch and Soda

Words and Music by Dave Guard

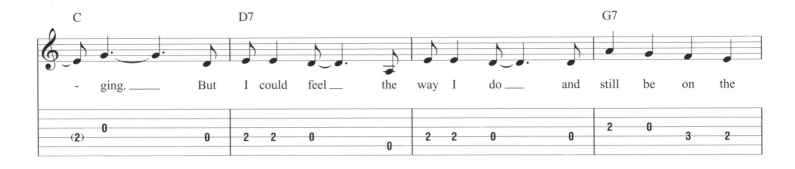

C   D7   G7

-ging. ___ But I could feel ___ the way I do ___ and still be on the

Verse

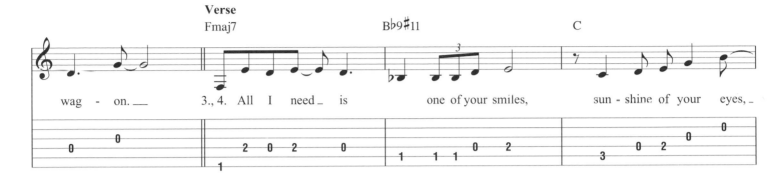

Fmaj7   Bb9#11   C

wag - on. ___   3., 4. All I need ___ is   one of your smiles,   sun - shine of your   eyes, ___

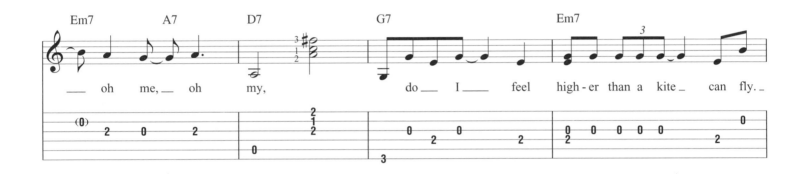

Em7   A7   D7   G7   Em7

___ oh me, ___ oh   my,   do ___ I ___ feel   high - er than a kite ___ can fly. ___

To Coda ⊕

A7   F   G7   C

___   Give me lov - in',   ba - by, I ___ feel high. ___

D.S. al Coda   ⊕ **Coda**

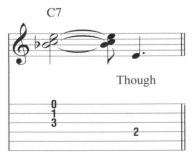

C7

Though

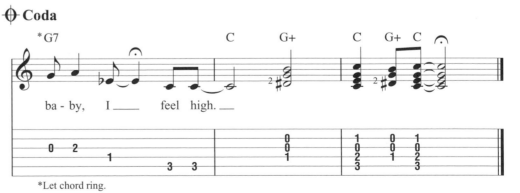

*G7   C   G+   C   G+   C

ba - by, I ___ feel high. ___

*Let chord ring.

Additional Lyrics

2. Dry martini, jigger of gin,
   Oh, what a spell you've got me in.
   Oh my, do I feel high.

The Sound of Silence

Words and Music by Paul Simon

*Capo VI

Strum Pattern: 3
Pick Pattern: 5

*Optional: To match recording, place capo at 6th fret.
**Use Pattern 10 for 2/4 meas.

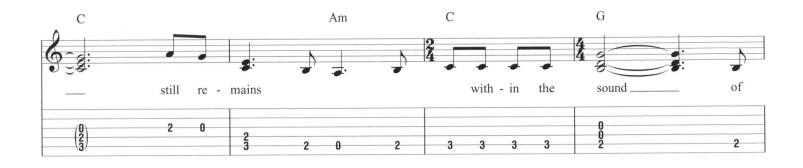

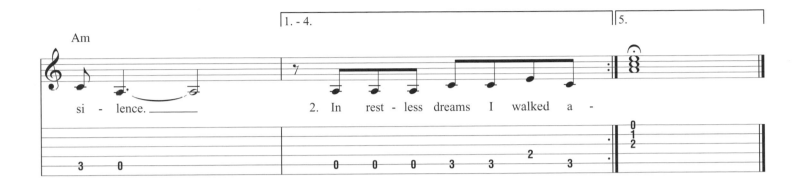

Additional Lyrics

2. In restless dreams I walked alone
   Narrow streets of cobblestone.
   'Neath the halo of a street lamp,
   I turned my collar to the cold and damp
   When my eyes were stabbed by the flash of a neon light
   That split the night
   And touched the sound of silence.

3. And in the naked light I saw
   Ten thousand people, maybe more.
   People talking without speaking,
   People hearing without list'ning.
   People writing songs that voices never shared
   And no one dared
   Disturb the sound of silence.

4. "Fools!" said I, "You do not know,
   Silence like a cancer grows.
   Hear my words that I might teach you.
   Take my arms that I might reach you."
   But my words like silent raindrops fell,
   And echoed in the wells of silence.

5. And the people bowed and prayed
   To the neon god they made.
   And the sign flashed out its warning
   In the words that it was forming.
   And the sign said, "The words of the prophets are written on the subway walls
   And tenement halls,
   And whispered in the sounds of silence."

Southern Cross

Words and Music by Stephen Stills, Richard Curtis and Michael Curtis

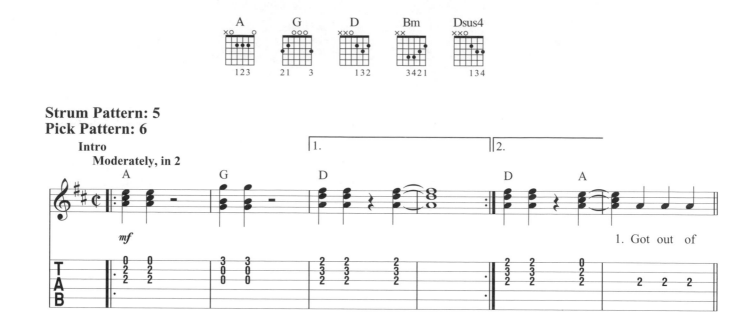

Strum Pattern: 5
Pick Pattern: 6

wind   on this hea-ding, lie ___ the Mar - que - sas. ___   We got   eight - y   feet _ of
4. See additional lyrics

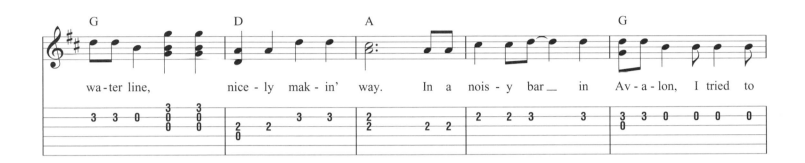

wa - ter line,   nice - ly mak - in' way.   In a   nois - y bar ___ in   Av - a - lon, I tried to

call   you,   but on the mid - night watch I   re - al - ized   why twice you ran   a - way. _

Pre-Chorus

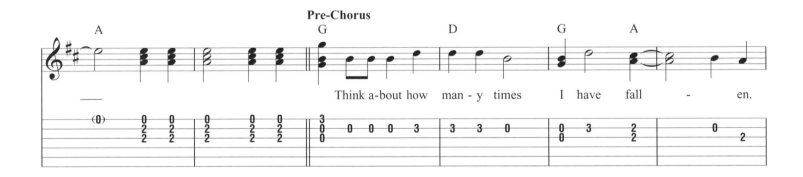

___   Think a - bout how man - y times   I have   fall ___ en.

___ Spir - its are   us - in' me;   larg - er voic - es   call - in'.   What heav - en brought

you and me can-not be for-got - ten. I have been a-

Chorus

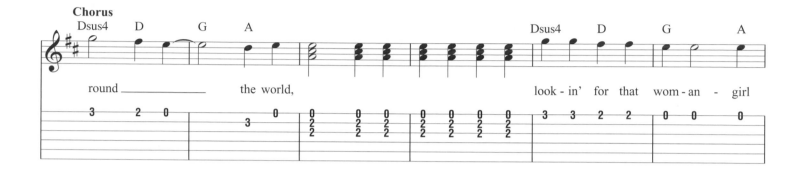

round _____ the world, look - in' for that wom - an - girl

who knows love can en - dure. And you know it will. _

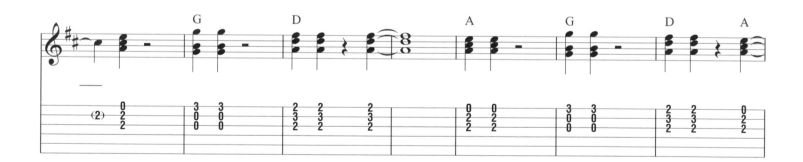

Verse

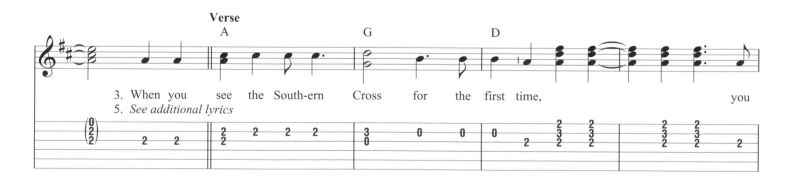

3. When you see the South-ern Cross for the first time, you
5. *See additional lyrics*

92

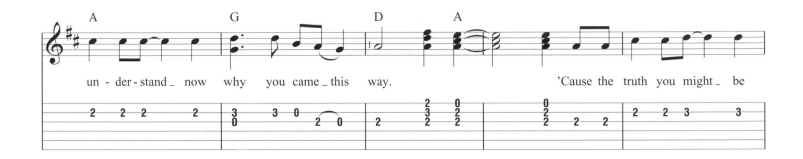

un-der-stand ___ now why you came ___ this way. 'Cause the truth you might ___ be

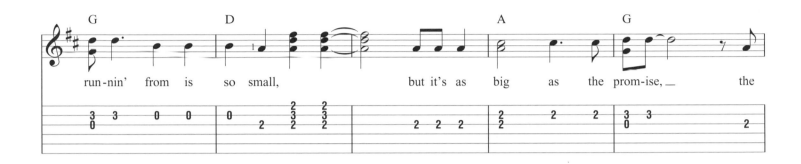

run-nin' from is so small, but it's as big as the prom-ise, ___ the

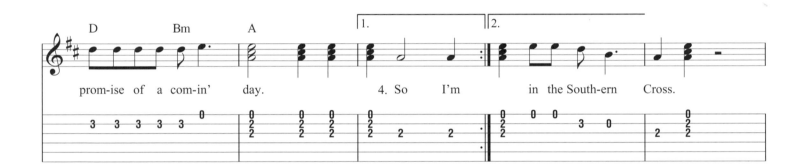

prom-ise of a com-in' day. 4. So I'm in the South-ern Cross.

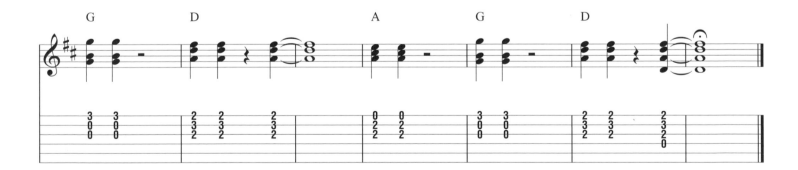

Additional Lyrics

4. So I'm sailing for tomorrow. My dreams are a-dying.
And my love is an anchor tied to you, tied with a silver chain.
I have my ship, and all her flags are a-flying.
She is all that I have left, and music is her name.

5. So we cheated and we lied and we tested.
And we never failed to fail; it was the easiest thing to do.
You will survive being bested.
Somebody fine will come along, make me forget about loving you
In the Southern Cross.

Sunshine
(Go Away Today)

Written by Jonathan Edwards

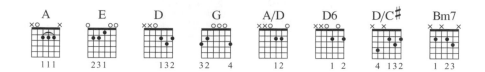

*Capo I

Strum Pattern: 1
Pick Pattern: 3

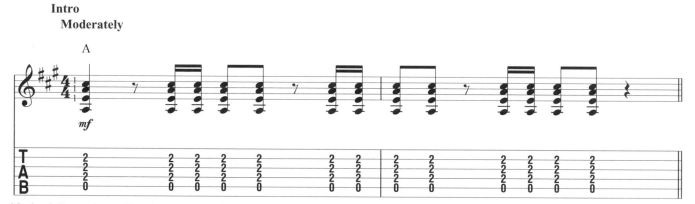

*Optional: To match recording, place capo at 1st fret.

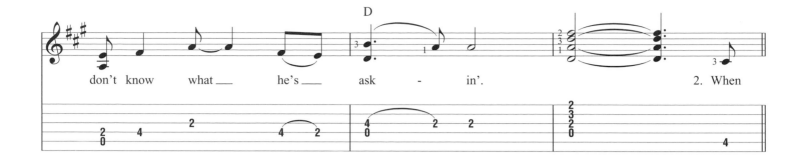

don't know what ___ he's ___ ask - in'. 2. When

𝄋 Verse

he tells me ___ I bet - ter get in line, ___ I can't hear what ___ he's
4., 5. *See additional lyrics*

say - in'. ___ When I grow up, ___ I'm gon - na make it mine, ___ or

3rd time, To Coda 𝄌

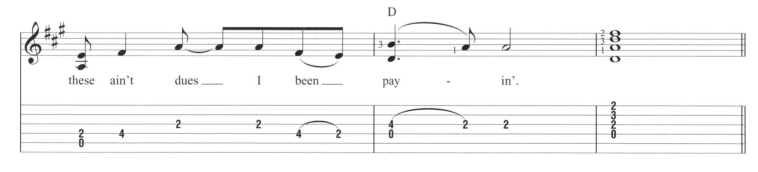

these ain't dues ___ I been ___ pay - in'.

Chorus

How much does it ___ cost? ___ I'll buy ___ it. The time is all ___ we've ___ lost. ___

95

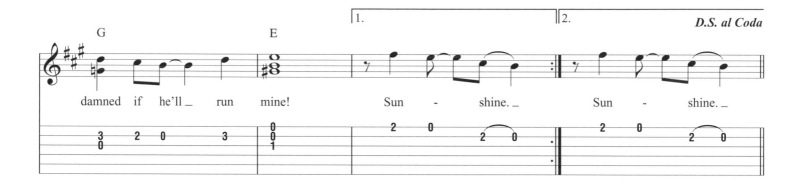

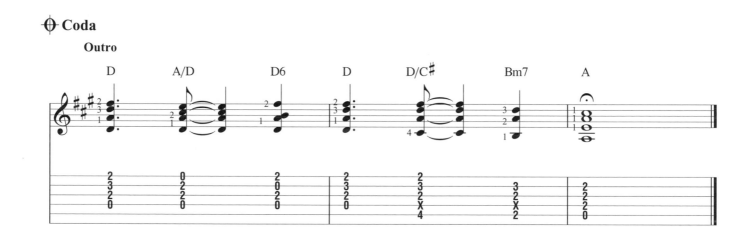

Additional Lyrics

4. Workin' starts to make me wonder where
   The fruits of what I do are goin'.
   He says in love and war, all is fair.
   But he's got cards he ain't showin'.

5. Sunshine come on back another day.
   I promise you I'll be singin'.
   This old world, she's gonna turn around.
   Brand-new bells will be ringin'.

Take Me Home, Country Roads

Words and Music by John Denver, Bill Danoff and Taffy Nivert

*Optional: To match recording, place capo at 2nd fret.

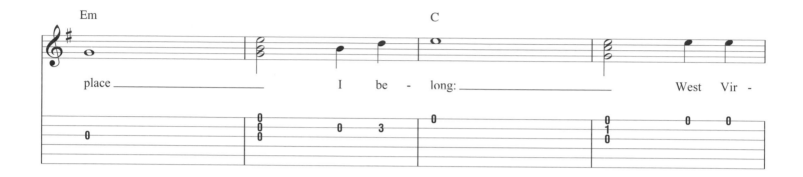

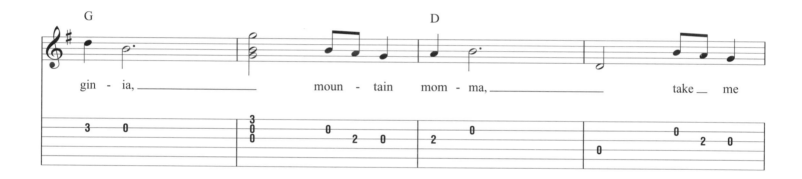

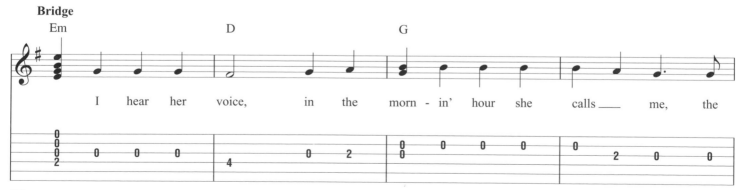

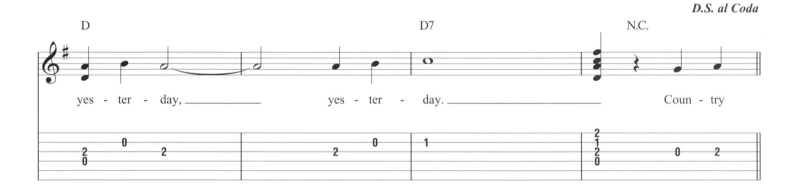

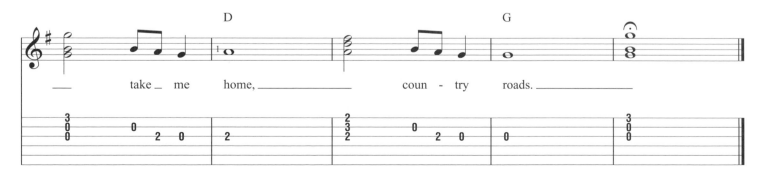

This Land Is Your Land

Words and Music by Woody Guthrie

this land was made for you and me. This land is

Chorus

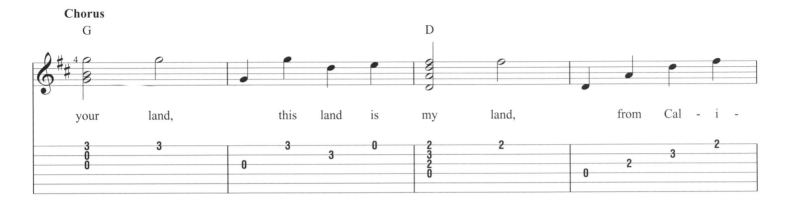

your land, this land is my land, from Cal - i -

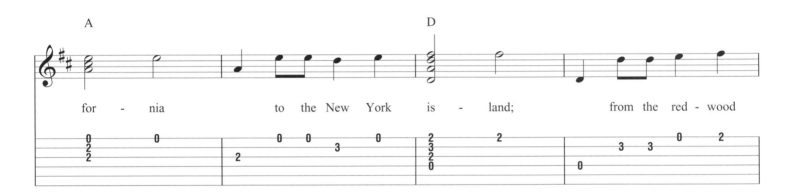

for - nia to the New York is - land; from the red - wood

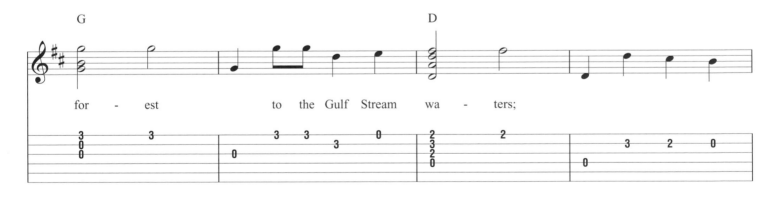

for - est to the Gulf Stream wa - ters;

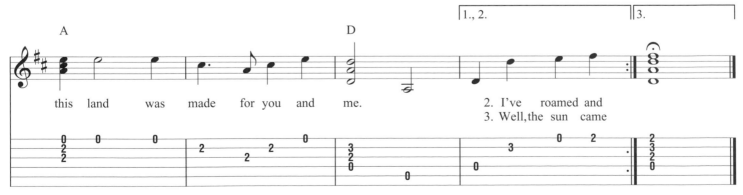

this land was made for you and me.
2. I've roamed and
3. Well, the sun came

Those Were the Days

Words and Music by Gene Raskin

*Capo II

Strum Pattern: 1
Pick Pattern: 5

Intro
Moderately slow

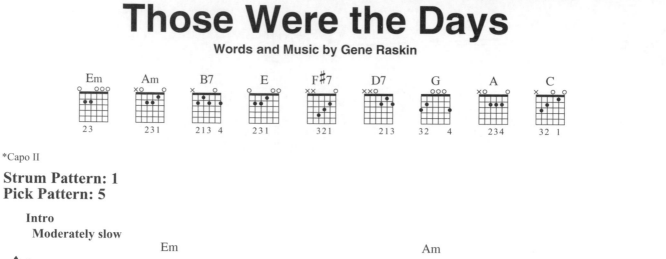

*To match recording, place capo at 2nd fret.

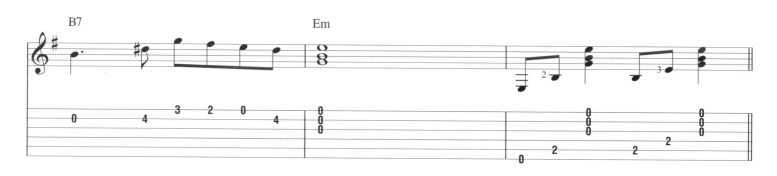

%Verse

1. Once up-on a time there was a tav-ern where we used to raise a glass or
2., 3., 4. *See additional lyrics*

**Sung one octave higher throughout.

two. _____ Re-mem-ber how we laughed a-way the ho-urs,

think of all the great things we would do. Those were the

Chorus

days, my friend. _ We thought they'd nev - er end. _ We'd sing and dance for - ev - er and a

day. We'd live the life we choose, _ we'd fight and nev - er lose, _ { 1. for we were
2., 3. those were the

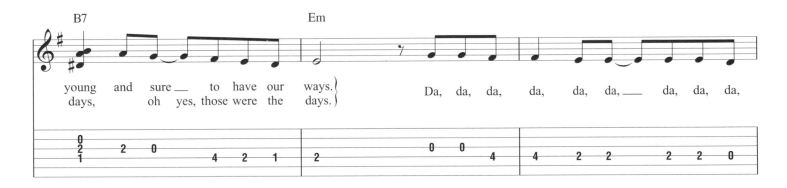

young and sure _ to have our ways. } Da, da, da, da, da, da, _ da, da, da,
days, oh yes, those were the days. }

1., 2.

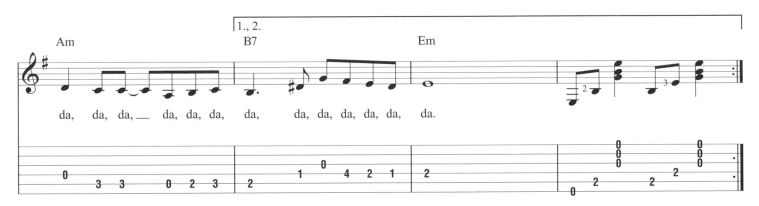

da, da, da, _ da, da, da, da, da, da, da, da, da, da.

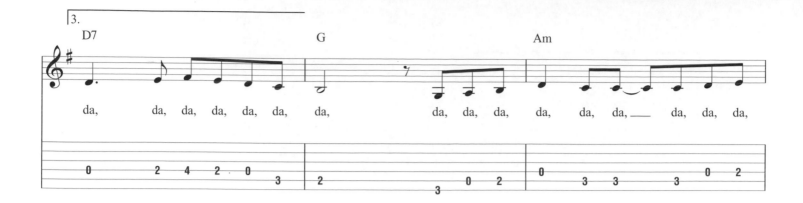

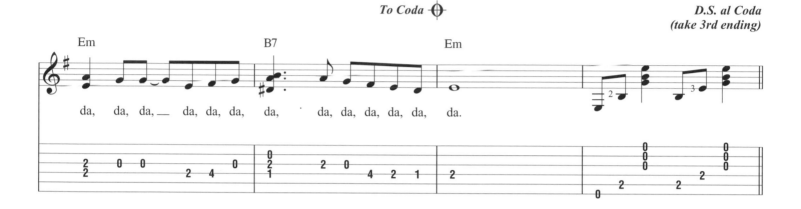

Additional Lyrics

2. Then the busy years went rushing by us.
   We lost our starry notions on the way.
   If by chance I'd see you in the tavern,
   We'd smile at one another and we'd say:

3. Just tonight, I stood before the tavern.
   Nothing seemed the way it used to be.
   In the glass I saw a strange reflection.
   Was that lonely woman really me?

4. Through the door there came familiar laughter.
   I saw your face and heard you call my name.
   Oh, my friend, we're older but no wiser,
   For in our hearts the dreams are still the same.

Turn! Turn! Turn!
(To Everything There Is a Season)

Words from the Book of Ecclesiastes
Adaptation and Music by Pete Seeger

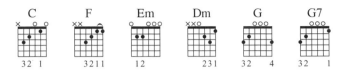

Strum Pattern: 4, 5
Pick Pattern: 4, 5

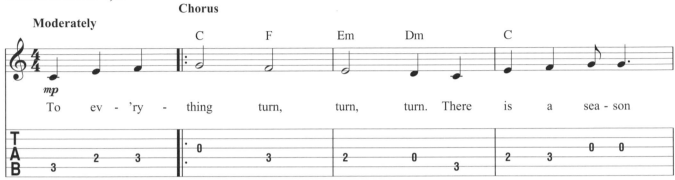

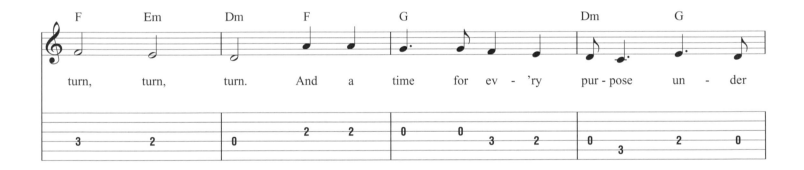

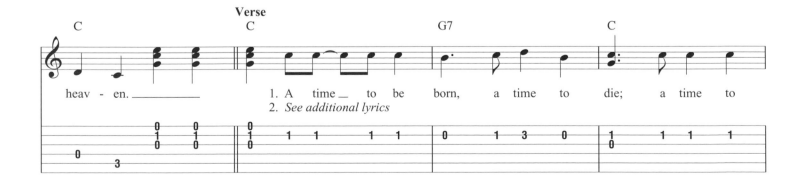

plant, a time to reap; a time to kill, a time to heal; a time to

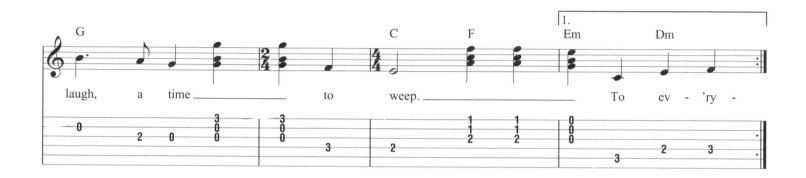

laugh, a time _____ to weep. _____ To ev - 'ry -

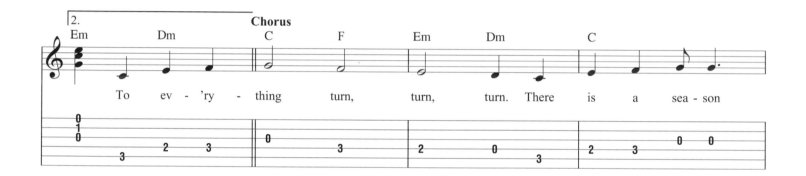

To ev - 'ry - thing turn, turn, turn. There is a sea - son

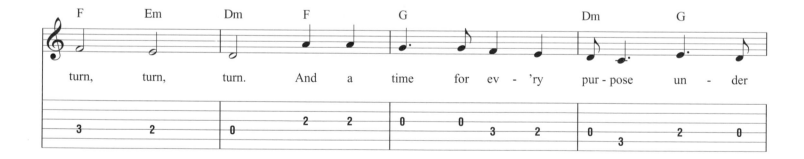

turn, turn, turn. And a time for ev - 'ry pur - pose un - der

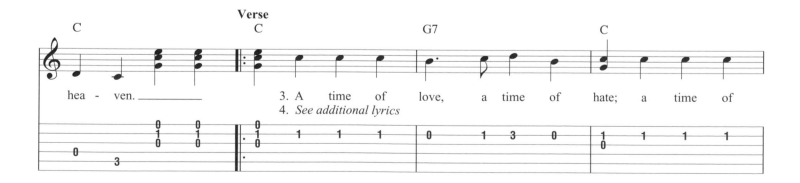

hea - ven. _____ 3. A time of love, a time of hate; a time of
4. *See additional lyrics*

106

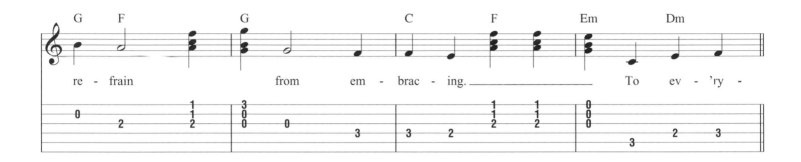

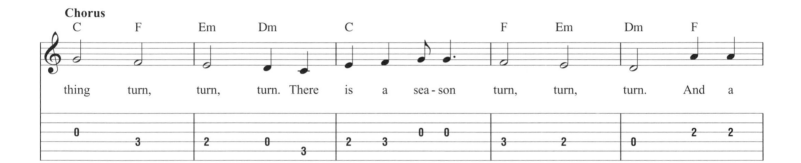

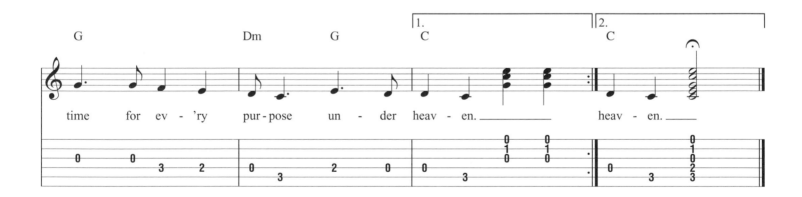

Additional Lyrics

2. A time to build up, a time to break down;
   A time to dance, a time to mourn;
   A time to cast away stones,
   A time to gather stones together.

4. A time to gain, a time to lose;
   A time to bend, a time to sew;
   A time to love, a time to hate;
   A time for peace, I swear it's not too late.

Time in a Bottle

Words and Music by Jim Croce

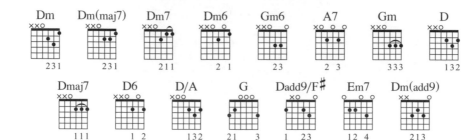

Strum Pattern: 9
Pick Pattern: 9

Intro
Moderately

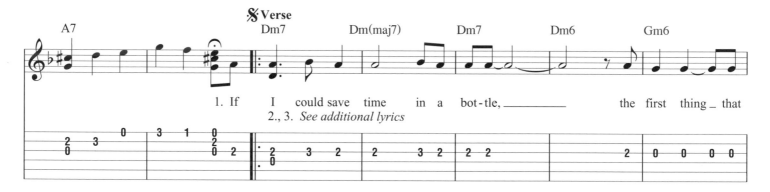

1. If I could save time in a bot-tle, _____ the first thing _ that
2., 3. *See additional lyrics*

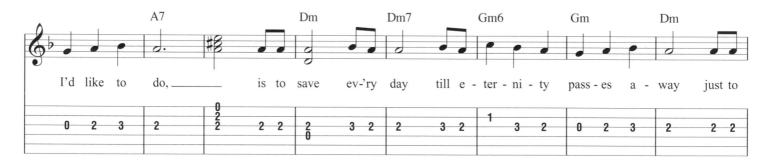

I'd like to do, _____ is to save ev-'ry day till e-ter-ni-ty pass-es a-way just to

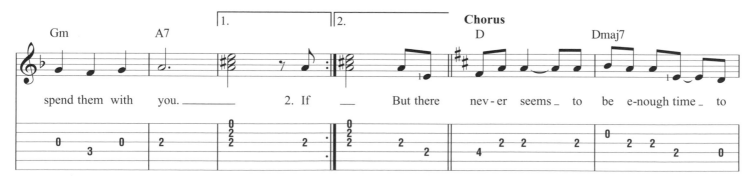

spend them with you. _____ 2. If ___ But there nev-er seems _ to be e-nough time _ to

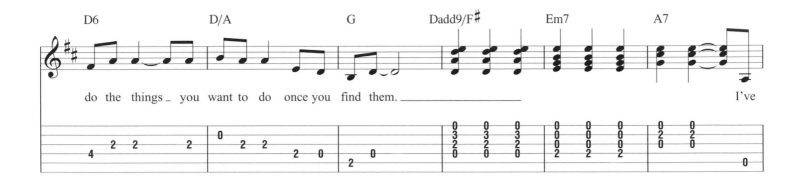

do the things _ you want to do once you find them. _____ I've

looked a - round _ e - nough to know _ that you're the one I want to go through time with.

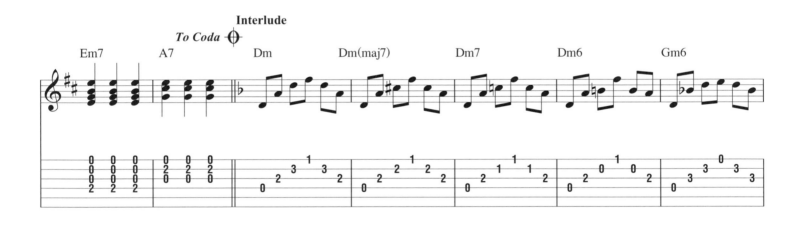

Interlude

To Coda ⊕

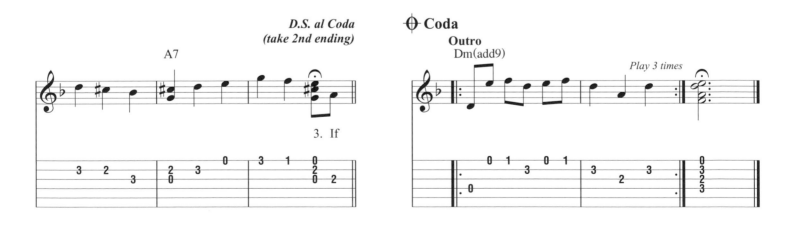

D.S. al Coda
(take 2nd ending)

3. If

⊕ **Coda**

Outro

Play 3 times

Additional Lyrics

2. If I could make days last forever,
   If words could make wishes come true,
   I'd save ev'ry day like a treasure, and then
   Again I would spend them with you.

3. If I had a box just for wishes,
   And dreams that had never come true,
   The box would be empty except for the mem'ry
   Of how they were answered by you.

Tom Dooley

Words and Music Collected, Adapted and Arranged by Frank Warner, John A. Lomax and Alan Lomax
From the singing of Frank Proffitt

Strum Pattern: 6
Pick Pattern: 2, 5

See additional lyrics

Hang down your head, Tom Doo-ley. Hang down your head and cry.

*Sung one octave lower throughout.

Hang down your head, Tom Doo-ley. Poor boy, you're bound to die. 1. I

Additional Lyrics

Intro Spoken: *Throughout history, there have been many songs written about the eternal triangle.*
                This next one tells the story of a Mr. Grayson, a beautiful woman, and a condemned man named Tom Dooley.
                When the sun rises tomorrow, Tom Dooley must hang.

2. This time tomorrow, reckon where I'll be?
    Hadn't a been for Grayson, I'd a been in Tennessee.

3. This time tomorrow, reckon where I'll be?
    Down in some lonesome valley, hangin' from a white oak tree.

Walk Right In

Words and Music by Gus Cannon and H. Woods

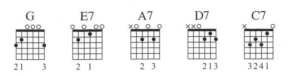

*Capo I

Strum Pattern: 3
Pick Pattern: 3

*Optional: To match recording, place capo at 1st fret.

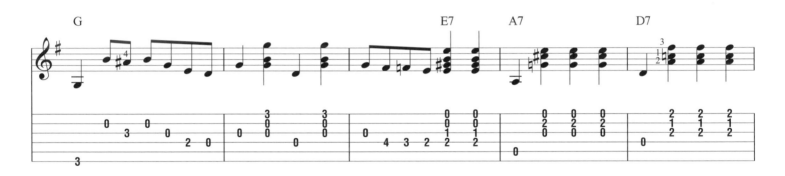

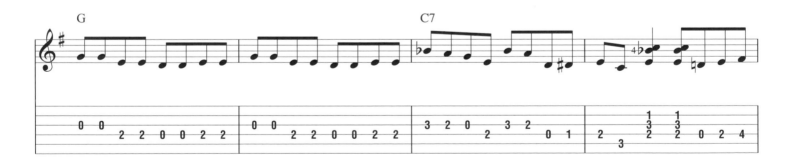

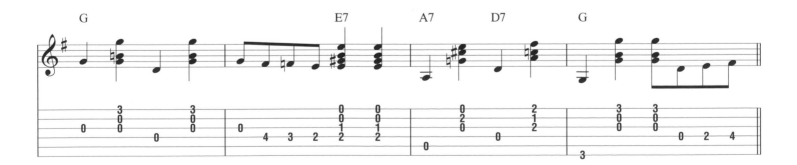

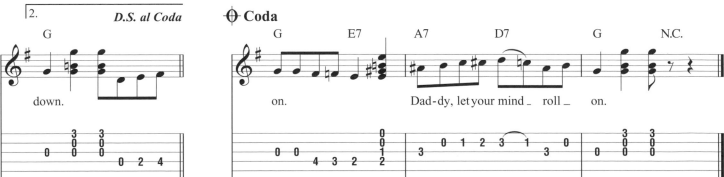

We Shall Overcome

Musical and Lyrical Adaptation by Zilphia Horton, Frank Hamilton, Guy Carawan and Pete Seeger
Inspired by African American Gospel Singing, members of the Food and Tobacco Workers Union,
Charleston, SC, and the southern Civil Rights Movement

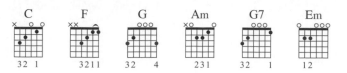

*Tune down 1/2 step:
(low to high) Eb-Ab-Db-Gb-Bb-Eb

Strum Pattern: 3
Pick Pattern: 5

Intro
Moderately

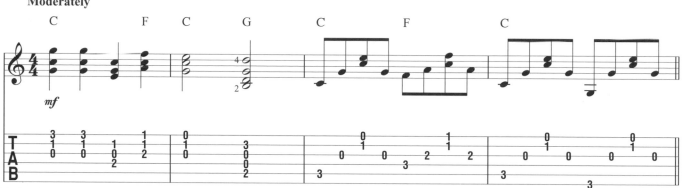

*Optional: To match recording, tune down 1/2 step.

Verse

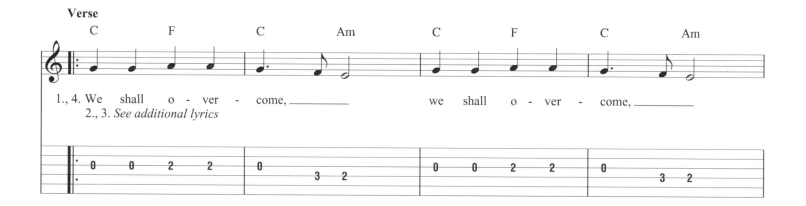

1., 4. We shall o - ver - come, _____ we shall o - ver - come, _____
2., 3. *See additional lyrics*

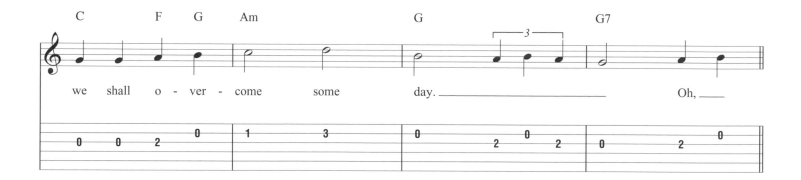

we shall o - ver - come some day. _____ Oh, ____

Chorus

deep in my heart I do be -

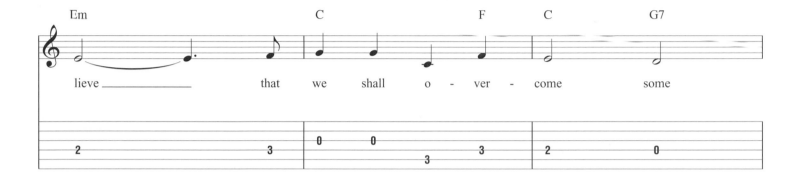

lieve _____ that we shall o - ver - come some

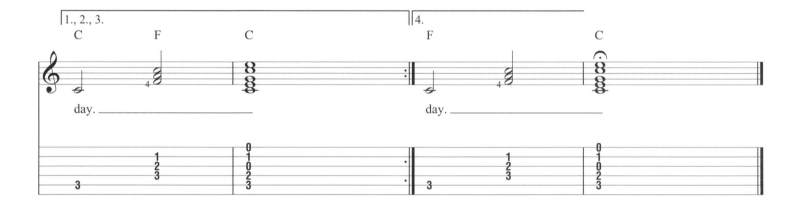

day. _____ day. _____

Additional Lyrics

2. We'll walk hand in hand,
   We'll walk hand in hand,
   We'll walk hand in hand some day.

3. We are not afraid,
   We are not afraid,
   We are not afraid today.

Where Have All the Flowers Gone?

Words and Music by Pete Seeger

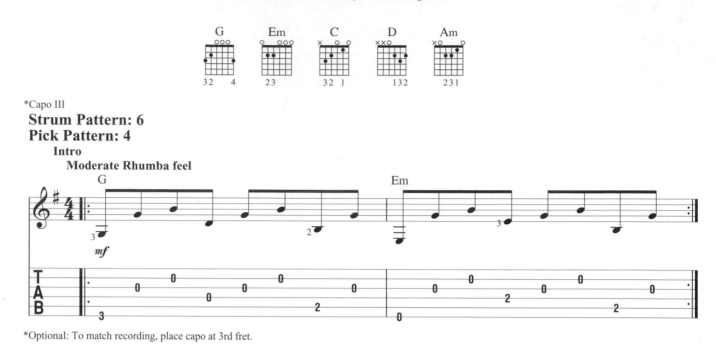

*Capo III

Strum Pattern: 6
Pick Pattern: 4

Intro
Moderate Rhumba feel

*Optional: To match recording, place capo at 3rd fret.

Verse

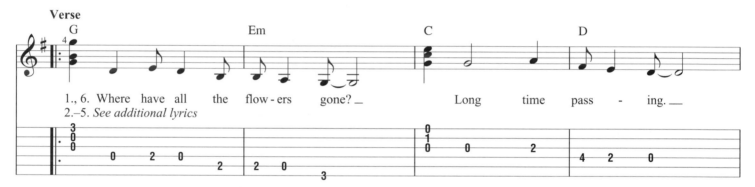

1., 6. Where have all the flow-ers gone? __ Long time pass - ing. __
2.–5. *See additional lyrics*

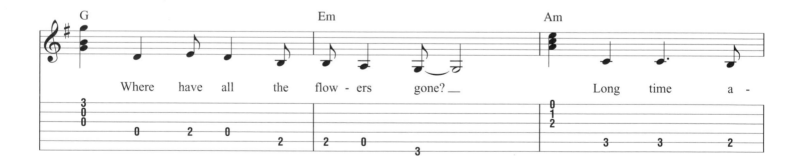

Where have all the flow-ers gone? __ Long time a -

go. _____ Where have all the flow-ers gone? __

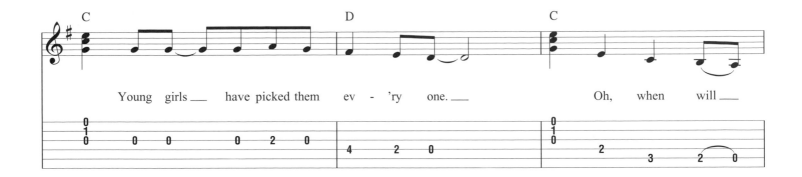

Young girls___ have picked them ev - 'ry one.___ Oh, when will___

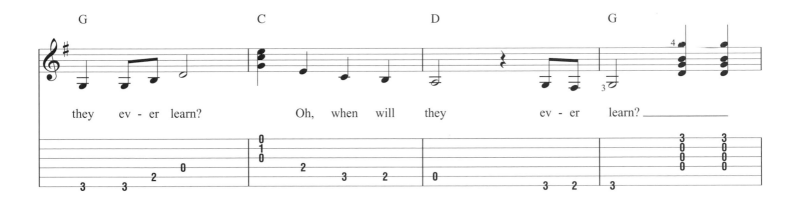

they ev - er learn? Oh, when will they ev - er learn?___

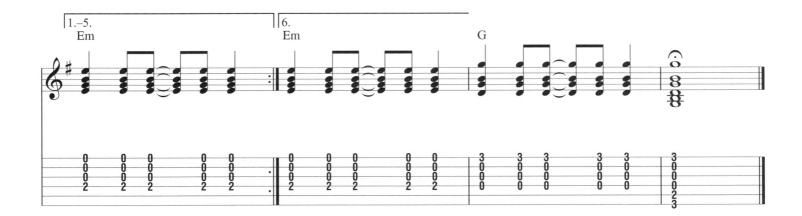

Additional Lyrics

2. Where have all the young girls gone?
   Long time passing.
   Where have all the young girls gone?
   Long time ago.
   Where have all the young girls gone?
   Gone for husbands, every one.
   Oh, when will they ever learn?
   Oh, when will they ever learn?

3. Where have all the husbands gone?
   Long time passing.
   Where have all the husbands gone?
   Long time ago.
   Where have all the husbands gone?
   Gone for soldiers, every one.
   Oh, when will they ever learn?
   Oh, when will they ever learn?

4. Where have all the soldiers gone?
   Long time passing.
   Where have all the soldiers gone?
   Long time ago.
   Where have all the soldiers gone?
   Gone to graveyards, every one.
   Oh, when will they ever learn?
   Oh, when will they ever learn?

5. Where have all the graveyards gone?
   Long time passing.
   Where have all the graveyards gone?
   Long time ago.
   Where have all the graveyards gone?
   Gone to flowers, every one.
   Oh, when will they ever learn?
   Oh, when will they ever learn?

Yesterday

Words and Music by John Lennon and Paul McCartney

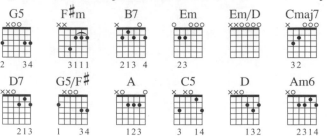

*Tune down 1 step:
(low to high) D-G-C-F-A-D

Strum Pattern: 3
Pick Pattern: 3

Intro
Moderately

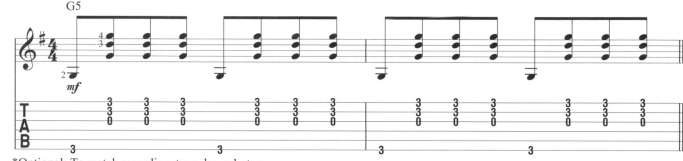

*Optional: To match recording, tune down 1 step.

Verse

1. Yes - ter - day,   all my trou - bles seemed so   far   a - way. ___
2. Sud - den - ly,   I'm not half the man I   used   to be. ___

Now   it   looks as though they're   here   to   stay. ___   Oh,   I   be - lieve   in
There's a   shad - ow   hang - ing   o - ver   me. ___   Oh,   yes - ter - day   came

Bridge

yes - ter - day. ___   Why   she   had   to   go,   I   don't
sud - den - ly. ___

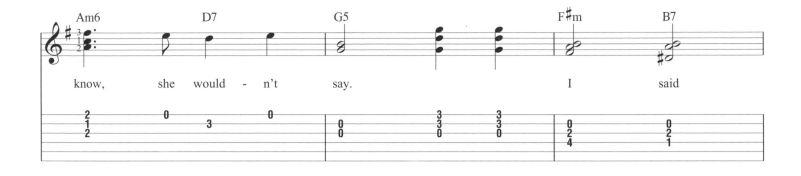

know,   she   would – n't   say.   I   said

some – thing   wrong,   now I   long   for   yes – ter – day. _____

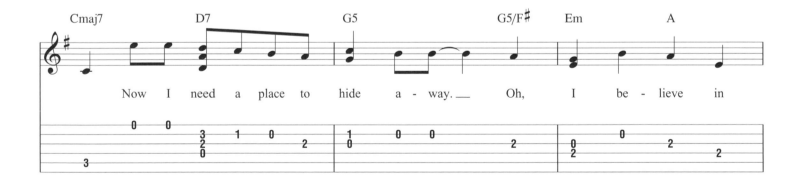

Verse

3., 4. Yes – ter – day,   love   was such an   eas – y   game   to   play. __

Now   I   need   a   place   to   hide   a – way. __   Oh,   I   be – lieve   in

Outro

yes – ter – day. __   Mm. _____

The Weight

By J.R. Robertson

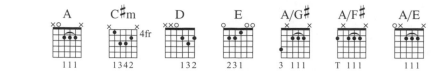

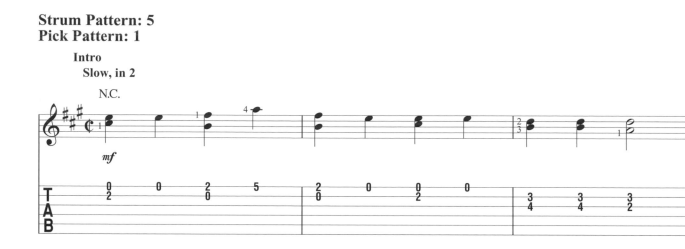

Strum Pattern: 5
Pick Pattern: 1

Intro
Slow, in 2

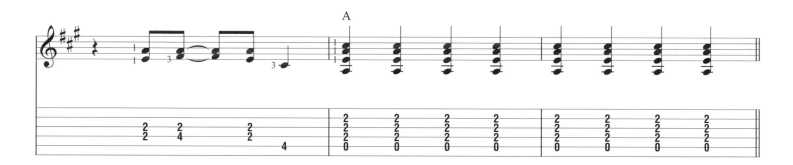

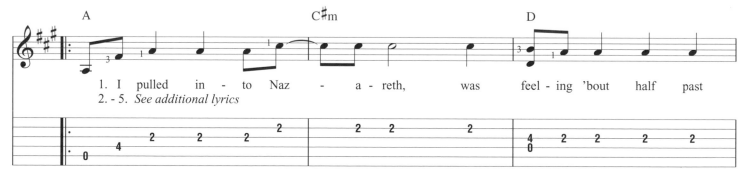

Verse

1. I pulled in to Naz - a - reth, was feel - ing 'bout half past
2. - 5. *See additional lyrics*

dead.   I just need some place _____ where

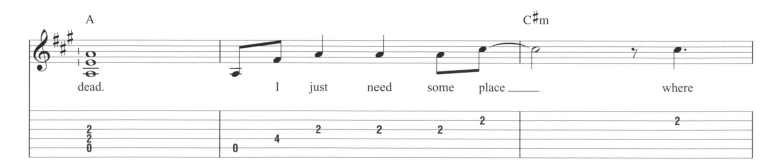

I can lay ___ my head. _____ "Hey, mis - ter, can you

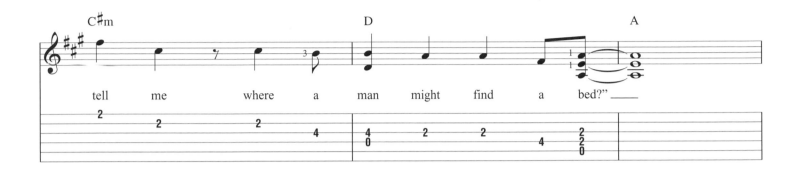

tell me where a man might find a bed?" ___

He just grinned and shook my hand; _ "No," was all ___ he said.

Chorus

Take a load off, Fan - ny. Take a load for

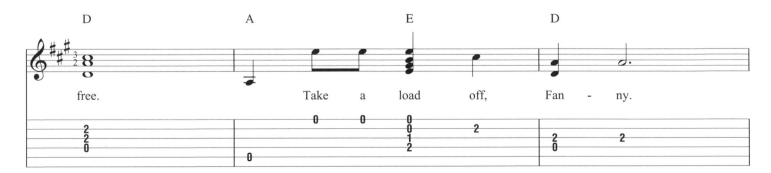

free. Take a load off, Fan - ny.

*Use Pattern 10.

**T = Thumb on 6th string

Additional Lyrics

2. I picked up my bag, I went lookin' for a place to hide,
   When I saw ol' Carmen and the Devil walkin' side by side.
   I said, "Hey, Carmen, come on, let's go downtown."
   She said, "I gotta go, but my friend can stick around."

3. Go down, Miss Moses, there's nothing you can say.
   It's just ol' Luke, and Luke's waitin' on a judgment day.
   "Well, Luke, my friend, what about young Anna Lee?"
   He said, "Do me a favor, son, won't you stay and keep Anna Lee company?"

4. Crazy Chester followed me and he caught me in the fog.
   He said, "I will fix your rack if you'll take Jack, my dog."
   I said, "Wait a minute, Chester, you know I'm a peaceful man."
   He said, "That's okay, boy, won't you feed him when you can?"

5. Catch a cannonball, now, to take me down the line.
   My bag is sinking low, and I do believe it's time
   To get back to Miss Fanny; you know she's the only one
   Who sent me here with her regards for ev'ryone.

EASY GUITAR
WITH NOTES & TAB

This series features simplified arrangements with notes, tab, chord charts, and strum and pick patterns.

MIXED FOLIOS

00702287	Acoustic	$19.99
00702002	Acoustic Rock Hits for Easy Guitar	$15.99
00702166	All-Time Best Guitar Collection	$19.99
00702232	Best Acoustic Songs for Easy Guitar	$16.99
00119835	Best Children's Songs	$16.99
00703055	The Big Book of Nursery Rhymes & Children's Songs	$16.99
00698978	Big Christmas Collection	$19.99
00702394	Bluegrass Songs for Easy Guitar	$15.99
00289632	Bohemian Rhapsody	$19.99
00703387	Celtic Classics	$16.99
00224808	Chart Hits of 2016-2017	$14.99
00267383	Chart Hits of 2017-2018	$14.99
00334293	Chart Hits of 2019-2020	$16.99
00403479	Chart Hits of 2021-2022	$16.99
00702149	Children's Christian Songbook	$9.99
00702028	Christmas Classics	$8.99
00101779	Christmas Guitar	$14.99
00702141	Classic Rock	$8.95
00159642	Classical Melodies	$12.99
00253933	Disney/Pixar's Coco	$16.99
00702203	CMT's 100 Greatest Country Songs	$34.99
00702283	The Contemporary Christian Collection	$16.99

00196954	Contemporary Disney	$19.99
00702239	Country Classics for Easy Guitar	$24.99
00702257	Easy Acoustic Guitar Songs	$17.99
00702041	Favorite Hymns for Easy Guitar	$12.99
00222701	Folk Pop Songs	$17.99
00126894	Frozen	$14.99
00333922	Frozen 2	$14.99
00702286	Glee	$16.99
00702160	The Great American Country Songbook	$19.99
00702148	Great American Gospel for Guitar	$14.99
00702050	Great Classical Themes for Easy Guitar	$9.99
00275088	The Greatest Showman	$17.99
00148030	Halloween Guitar Songs	$14.99
00702273	Irish Songs	$14.99
00192503	Jazz Classics for Easy Guitar	$16.99
00702275	Jazz Favorites for Easy Guitar	$17.99
00702274	Jazz Standards for Easy Guitar	$19.99
00702162	Jumbo Easy Guitar Songbook	$24.99
00232285	La La Land	$16.99
00702258	Legends of Rock	$14.99
00702189	MTV's 100 Greatest Pop Songs	$34.99
00702272	1950s Rock	$16.99
00702271	1960s Rock	$16.99
00702270	1970s Rock	$24.99
00702269	1980s Rock	$16.99

00702268	1990s Rock	$24.99
00369043	Rock Songs for Kids	$14.99
00109725	Once	$14.99
00702187	Selections from O Brother Where Art Thou?	$19.99
00702178	100 Songs for Kids	$16.99
00702515	Pirates of the Caribbean	$17.99
00702125	Praise and Worship for Guitar	$14.99
00287930	Songs from *A Star Is Born, The Greatest Showman, La La Land,* and More Movie Musicals	$16.99
00702285	Southern Rock Hits	$12.99
00156420	Star Wars Music	$16.99
00121535	30 Easy Celtic Guitar Solos	$16.99
00244654	Top Hits of 2017	$14.99
00283786	Top Hits of 2018	$14.99
00302269	Top Hits of 2019	$14.99
00355779	Top Hits of 2020	$14.99
00374083	Top Hits of 2021	$16.99
00702294	Top Worship Hits	$17.99
00702255	VH1's 100 Greatest Hard Rock Songs	$34.99
00702175	VH1's 100 Greatest Songs of Rock and Roll	$34.99
00702253	Wicked	$12.99

ARTIST COLLECTIONS

00702267	AC/DC for Easy Guitar	$16.99
00156221	Adele – 25	$16.99
00396889	Adele – 30	$19.99
00702040	Best of the Allman Brothers	$16.99
00702865	J.S. Bach for Easy Guitar	$15.99
00702169	Best of The Beach Boys	$16.99
00702292	The Beatles — 1	$22.99
00125796	Best of Chuck Berry	$16.99
00702201	The Essential Black Sabbath	$15.99
00702250	blink-182 — Greatest Hits	$17.99
02501615	Zac Brown Band — The Foundation	$17.99
02501621	Zac Brown Band — You Get What You Give	$16.99
00702043	Best of Johnny Cash	$17.99
00702090	Eric Clapton's Best	$16.99
00702086	Eric Clapton — from the Album Unplugged	$17.99
00702202	The Essential Eric Clapton	$17.99
00702053	Best of Patsy Cline	$17.99
00222697	Very Best of Coldplay – 2nd Edition	$17.99
00702229	The Very Best of Creedence Clearwater Revival	$16.99
00702145	Best of Jim Croce	$16.99
00702278	Crosby, Stills & Nash	$12.99
14042809	Bob Dylan	$15.99
00702276	Fleetwood Mac — Easy Guitar Collection	$17.99
00139462	The Very Best of Grateful Dead	$16.99
00702136	Best of Merle Haggard	$16.99
00702227	Jimi Hendrix — Smash Hits	$19.99
00702288	Best of Hillsong United	$12.99
00702236	Best of Antonio Carlos Jobim	$15.99

00702245	Elton John — Greatest Hits 1970–2002	$19.99
00129855	Jack Johnson	$17.99
00702204	Robert Johnson	$16.99
00702234	Selections from Toby Keith — 35 Biggest Hits	$12.95
00702003	Kiss	$16.99
00702216	Lynyrd Skynyrd	$17.99
00702182	The Essential Bob Marley	$16.99
00146081	Maroon 5	$14.99
00121925	Bruno Mars – Unorthodox Jukebox	$12.99
00702248	Paul McCartney — All the Best	$14.99
00125484	The Best of MercyMe	$12.99
00702209	Steve Miller Band — Young Hearts (Greatest Hits)	$12.95
00124167	Jason Mraz	$15.99
00702096	Best of Nirvana	$16.99
00702211	The Offspring — Greatest Hits	$17.99
00138026	One Direction	$17.99
00702030	Best of Roy Orbison	$17.99
00702144	Best of Ozzy Osbourne	$14.99
00702279	Tom Petty	$17.99
00102911	Pink Floyd	$17.99
00702139	Elvis Country Favorites	$19.99
00702293	The Very Best of Prince	$19.99
00699415	Best of Queen for Guitar	$16.99
00109279	Best of R.E.M.	$14.99
00702208	Red Hot Chili Peppers — Greatest Hits	$17.99
00198960	The Rolling Stones	$17.99
00174793	The Very Best of Santana	$16.99
00702196	Best of Bob Seger	$16.99
00146046	Ed Sheeran	$17.99

00702252	Frank Sinatra — Nothing But the Best	$12.99
00702010	Best of Rod Stewart	$17.99
00702049	Best of George Strait	$17.99
00702259	Taylor Swift for Easy Guitar	$15.99
00359800	Taylor Swift – Easy Guitar Anthology	$24.99
00702260	Taylor Swift — Fearless	$14.99
00139727	Taylor Swift — 1989	$19.99
00115960	Taylor Swift — Red	$16.99
00253667	Taylor Swift — Reputation	$17.99
00702290	Taylor Swift — Speak Now	$16.99
00232849	Chris Tomlin Collection – 2nd Edition	$14.99
00702226	Chris Tomlin — See the Morning	$12.95
00148643	Train	$14.99
00702427	U2 — 18 Singles	$19.99
00702108	Best of Stevie Ray Vaughan	$17.99
00279005	The Who	$14.99
00702123	Best of Hank Williams	$15.99
00194548	Best of John Williams	$14.99
00702228	Neil Young — Greatest Hits	$17.99
00119133	Neil Young — Harvest	$14.99

Prices, contents and availability subject to change without notice.

HAL•LEONARD®

Visit Hal Leonard online at **halleonard.com**

HAL•LEONARD GUITAR PLAY-ALONG

Complete song lists available online.

This series will help you play your favorite songs quickly and easily. Just follow the tab and listen to the audio to the hear how the guitar should sound, and then play along using the separate backing tracks. Audio files also include software to slow down the tempo without changing pitch. The melody and lyrics are included in the book so that you can sing or simply follow along.

INCLUDES TAB

Prices, contents, and availability subject to change without notice.

HAL•LEONARD®
www.halleonard.com

0822

AUDIO ACCESS INCLUDED 🔊

The **Deluxe Guitar Play-Along®** series will help you play songs faster than ever before! Accurate, easy-to-read guitar tab and professional, customizable audio for 15 songs. The interactive, online audio interface includes tempo/pitch control, looping, buttons to turn instruments on or off, and guitar tab with follow-along marker.

The price of each book includes access to audio tracks online using the unique code inside. The tracks can also be downloaded and played offline. These books include *PLAYBACK+*, a multi-functional audio player that allows you to slow down audio, change pitch, set loop points, and pan left or right – available exclusively from Hal Leonard.

  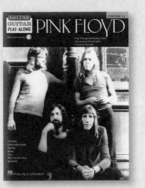  

1. TOP ROCK HITS
Basket Case • Black Hole Sun • Come As You Are • Do I Wanna Know? • Gold on the Ceiling • Heaven • How You Remind Me • Kryptonite • No One Knows • Plush • The Pretender • Seven Nation Army • Smooth • Under the Bridge • Yellow Ledbetter. 00244758

2. REALLY EASY SONGS
Californication • Free Fallin' • Hey Joe • Highway to Hell • I Love Rock 'N Roll • Knockin' on Heaven's Door • La Bamba • Oh, Pretty Woman • Should I Stay or Should I Go • Smells Like Teen Spirit. • and more. 00244877

3. ACOUSTIC SONGS
All Apologies • Banana Pancakes • Crash Into Me • Good Riddance (Time of Your Life) • Hallelujah • Hey There Delilah • Ho Hey • I Will Wait • I'm Yours • Iris • More Than Words • No Such Thing • Photograph • What I Got • Wonderwall. 00244709

4. THE BEATLES
All My Loving • And I Love Her • Back in the U.S.S.R. • Don't Let Me Down • Get Back • A Hard Day's Night • Here Comes the Sun • I Will • In My Life • Let It Be • Michelle • Paperback Writer • Revolution • While My Guitar Gently Weeps • Yesterday. 00244968

5. BLUES STANDARDS
Crosscut Saw • Double Trouble • Every Day I Have the Blues • Going Down • I'm Tore Down • I'm Your Hoochie Coochie Man • Killing Floor • Let Me Love You Baby • Pride and Joy • Sweet Home Chicago • and more. 00245090

6. RED HOT CHILI PEPPERS
The Adventures of Rain Dance Maggie • Breaking the Girl • Can't Stop • Dani California • Dark Necessities • Give It Away • My Friends • Otherside • Road Trippin' • Scar Tissue • Snow (Hey Oh) • Suck My Kiss • Tell Me Baby • Under the Bridge • The Zephyr Song. 00245089

7. CLASSIC ROCK
Baba O'Riley • Born to Be Wild • Comfortably Numb • Dream On • Fortunate Son • Heartbreaker • Hotel California • Jet Airliner • More Than a Feeling • Old Time Rock & Roll • Rhiannon • Runnin' Down a Dream • Start Me Up • Sultans of Swing • Sweet Home Alabama. 00248381

8. OZZY OSBOURNE
Bark at the Moon • Close My Eyes Forever • Crazy Train • Dreamer • Mama, I'm Coming Home • No More Tears • Over the Mountain • Perry Mason • Rock 'N Roll Rebel • Shot in the Dark • and more. 00248413

9. ED SHEERAN
The A Team • All of the Stars • Castle on the Hill • Don't • Drunk • Galway Girl • Give Me Love • How Would You Feel (Paean) • I See Fire • Lego House • Make It Rain • Perfect • Photograph • Shape of You • Thinking Out Loud. 00248439

10. CHRISTMAS SONGS
Blue Christmas • Christmas Time Is Here • Do You Hear What I Hear • Feliz Navidad • Have Yourself a Merry Little Christmas • I'll Be Home for Christmas • Little Saint Nick • Please Come Home for Christmas • Santa Baby • White Christmas • Winter Wonderland • and more. 00278088

11. PINK FLOYD
Another Brick in the Wall, Part 2 • Brain Damage • Breathe • Comfortably Numb • Goodbye Blue Sky • Have a Cigar • Hey You • Learning to Fly • Money • Mother • Run like Hell • Time • Welcome to the Machine • Wish You Were Here • Young Lust. 00278487

12. THREE-CHORD SONGS
Ain't No Sunshine • Bad Moon Rising • Beverly Hills • Evil Ways • Just the Way You Are • Ring of Fire • Twist and Shout • What I Got • What's Up • and more. 00278488

13. FOUR-CHORD SONGS
Chasing Cars • Cruise • Demons • Hand in My Pocket • Hey, Soul Sister • Hey Ya! • If I Had $1,000,000 • Riptide • Rude • Save Tonight • Steal My Girl • Steal My Kisses • 3 AM • Toes • Zombie. 00287263

14. BOB SEGER
Against the Wind • Feel like a Number • The Fire down Below • Fire Lake • Her Strut • Hollywood Nights • Like a Rock • Mainstreet • Night Moves • Old Time Rock & Roll • Rock and Roll Never Forgets • Still the Same • Sunspot Baby • Turn the Page • You'll Accomp'ny Me. 00287279

15. METAL ANTHOLOGY
Ace of Spades • The Devil in I • Down with the Sickness • Hallowed Be Thy Name • Master of Puppets • No More Tears • Painkiller • Rainbow in the Dark • Sober • Walk • War Pigs (Interpolating Luke's Wall) • and more. 00287269

18. KISS
Christine Sixteen • Cold Gin • Detroit Rock City • Deuce • Firehouse • God of Thunder • Heaven's on Fire • I Stole Your Love • I Was Made for Lovin' You • Lick It Up • Love Gun • Rock and Roll All Nite • Shock Me • Shout It Out Loud • Strutter. 00288989

19. CHRISTMAS CLASSICS
Away in a Manger • Deck the Hall • The First Noel • Go, Tell It on the Mountain • Hark! the Herald Angels Sing • It Came upon the Midnight Clear • Jingle Bells • O Holy Night • O Little Town of Bethlehem • Silent Night • and more. 00294776

21. NEIL YOUNG
Cowgirl in the Sand • Down by the River • Harvest Moon • Heart of Gold • Like a Hurricane • Old Man • Only Love Can Break Your Heart • Rockin' in the Free World • Southern Man • and more. 00322911

24. JIMI HENDRIX
Angel • Crosstown Traffic • Fire • Foxey Lady • Freedom • Hear My Train a Comin' • Izabella • Little Wing • Manic Depression • Purple Haze • Red House • Star Spangled Banner (Instrumental) • Stone Free • Voodoo Child (Slight Return) • The Wind Cries Mary. 00324610

HAL•LEONARD®

Visit halleonard.com for more information

Prices, contents, and availability subject to change without notice.

Will Ackerman
00690016 The Will Ackerman Collection $24.99
Bryan Adams
00690501 Greatest Hits $24.99
Aerosmith
00690603 O Yeah! $29.99
Alice in Chains
00690178 Acoustic $22.99
00694865 Dirt $19.99
00660225 Facelift $19.99
00694925 Jar of Flies/Sap..........$19.99
00690387 Nothing Safe $24.99
All That Remains
00142819 The Order of Things..$22.99
Allman Brothers Band
00694932 Definitive Collection, Volume 1...................$29.99
00694933 Definitive Collection, Volume 2...................$27.99
00694934 Definitive Collection, Volume 3...................$29.99
Duane Allman
00690958 Guitar Anthology $29.99
Alter Bridge
00691071 AB III $29.99
00690945 Blackbird $24.99
00690755 One Day Remains......$24.99
Anthrax
00690849 Best of Anthrax..........$27.99
Arctic Monkeys
00123558 AM $24.99
Chet Atkins
00690158 Almost Alone.............$22.99
00694878 Vintage Fingerstyle..$22.99
Audioslave
00690609 Audioslave.................$24.99
00690884 Revelations................$19.95
Avenged Sevenfold
00690926 Avenged Sevenfold $24.99
00214869 Best of: 2005-2013 ..$29.99
00690820 City of Evil $27.99
00123216 Hail to the King $27.99
00691051 Nightmare $27.99
00222486 The Stage $29.99
00691065 Waking the Fallen......$24.99
The Avett Brothers
00123140 Guitar Collection $22.99
Randy Bachman
00694918 Guitar Collection $24.99
The Beatles
00690489 1 (Number Ones) $24.99
00694929 1962-1966 ....$27.99
00694930 1967-1970 ....$29.99
00694880 Abbey Road $19.99
00694832 Acoustic Guitar.........$27.99
00691066 Beatles for Sale $22.99
00690903 Capitol Albums Vol. 2 .$24.99
00691031 Help! $19.99
00694482 Let It Be $19.99
00691030 Magical Mystery Tour..$22.99
00691067 Meet the Beatles! $22.99
00691068 Please Please Me $22.99
00694891 Revolver....................$22.99
00691014 Rock Band $34.99
00694914 Rubber Soul...............$24.99
00694863 Sgt. Pepper's Lonely Hearts Club Band $22.99
00110193 Tomorrow Never Knows $22.99
00690110 White Album Book 1..$19.99
00690111 White Album Book 2..$19.99

The Beach Boys
00690503 Very Best $24.99
Beck
00690632 Beck – Sea Change ...$19.95
Jeff Beck
00691044 Best of Beck..............$24.99
00691042 Blow by Blow $22.99
00691041 Truth $19.99
00691043 Wired.........................$19.99
George Benson
00694884 Best of $22.99
Chuck Berry
00692385 Chuck Berry..............$24.99
Billy Talent
00690835 Billy Talent $22.99
00690879 Billy Talent II............$22.99
Black Crowes
00147787 Best of $24.99
The Black Keys
00129737 Turn Blue $22.99
Black Sabbath
00690149 Black Sabbath $19.99
00690901 Best of $22.99
00691010 Heaven and Hell $24.99
00690148 Master of Reality $19.99
00690142 Paranoid $19.99
00691045 Vol. 4 ....$22.99
00692200 We Sold Our Soul for Rock 'n' Roll $24.99
blink-182
00690389 Enema of the State $22.99
00690831 Greatest Hits..............$24.99
00691179 Neighborhoods...........$22.99
Michael Bloomfield
00148544 Guitar Anthology $24.99
Blue Öyster Cult
00690028 Cult Classics $22.99
Bon Jovi
00691074 Greatest Hits.............$24.99
Joe Bonamassa
00158600 Blues of Desperation $24.99
00139086 Different Shades of Blue $22.99
00198117 Muddy Wolf at Red Rocks................$24.99
00283540 Redemption $24.99
00358863 Royal Tea $24.99
Boston
00690913 Boston.......................$22.99
00690829 Guitar Collection $24.99
David Bowie
00690491 Best of $22.99
Box Car Racer
00690583 Box Car Racer...........$19.95
Breaking Benjamin
00691023 Dear Agony $22.99
00690873 Phobia......................$22.99
Lenny Breau
00141446 Best of $19.99
Big Bill Broonzy
00286503 Guitar Collection $19.99
Roy Buchanan
00690168 Collection $24.99
Jeff Buckley
00690451 Collection $27.99
Bullet for My Valentine
00690957 Scream Aim Fire $22.99
00119629 Temper Temper $22.99
Kenny Burrell
00690678 Best of $24.99
Cage the Elephant
00691077 Thank You, Happy Birthday $22.99

The Cars
00691159 Complete Greatest Hits.$24.99
Carter Family
00690261 Collection.................$19.99
Johnny Cash
00691079 Best of......................$24.99
Cheap Trick
00690043 Best of......................$24.99
Chicago
00690171 Definitive Guitar Collection $29.99
Chimaira
00691011 Guitar Collection $24.99
Charlie Christian
00690567 Definitive Collection ..$22.99
Eric Church
00101916 Chief $22.99
The Civil Wars
00129545 The Civil Wars $19.99
Eric Clapton
00690590 Anthology..................$34.99
00694896 Blues Breakers (with John Mayall) $19.99
00138731 The Breeze $24.99
00691055 Clapton $22.99
00690936 Complete Clapton $34.99
00690010 From the Cradle $24.99
00192383 I Still Do $19.99
00690363 Just One Night $27.99
00694873 Timepieces $19.95
00694869 Unplugged.................$24.99
00124873 Unplugged (Deluxe) ..$29.99
The Clash
00690162 Best of......................$22.99
Coheed & Cambria
00690828 IV................................$24.99
00139967 In Keeping Secrets of Silent Earth: 3 ....$24.99
Coldplay
00130786 Ghost Stories.............$19.99
Collective Soul
00690855 Best of $19.95
Jessee Cook
00141704 Works Vol. 1 ....$22.99
Alice Cooper
00691091 Best of......................$24.99
Counting Crows
00694940 August & Everything After.........$22.99
Robert Cray
00127184 Best of $19.99
Cream
00694840 Disraeli Gears $24.99
Creed
00288787 Greatest Hits.............$22.99
Creedence Clearwater Revival
00690819 Best of......................$27.99
Jim Croce
00690648 The Very Best $19.99
Steve Cropper
00690572 Soul Man $22.99
Crosby, Stills & Nash
00690613 Best of......................$29.99
Cry of Love
00691171 Brother $22.99
Dick Dale
00690637 Best of......................$22.99
Death Cab for Cutie
00690967 Narrow Stairs $22.99
Deep Purple
00690289 Best of......................$22.99
00690288 Machine Head $19.99

Def Leppard
00690784 Best of......................$24.99
Derek and the Dominos
00694831 Layla & Other Assorted Love Songs..$24.99
Ani DiFranco
00690384 Best of......................$19.95
Dinosaur Jr.
00690979 Best of......................$22.99
The Doors
00690347 Anthology...................$22.95
00690348 Essential Collection ...$16.95
Dream Theater
00160579 The Astonishing $24.99
00122443 Dream Theater $29.99
00291164 Distance Over Time ..$24.99
Eagles
00278631 Their Greatest Hits 1971-1975.........$22.99
00278632 Very Best of..............$39.99
Duane Eddy
00690250 Best of......................$24.99
Tommy Emmanuel
00147067 All I Want for Christmas..................$19.99
00690909 Best of $27.99
00172824 It's Never Too Late $22.99
00139220 Little by Little $24.99
Melissa Etheridge
00690555 Best of......................$19.95
Evanescence
00691186 Evanescence..............$22.99
Extreme
00690515 Pornograffitti $24.99
John Fahey
00150257 Guitar Anthology $24.99
Tal Farlow
00125661 Best of......................$19.99
Five Finger Death Punch
00691009 5 Finger Death Punch $24.99
00691181 American Capitalism..$22.99
00128917 Wrong Side of Heaven & Righteous Side of Hell.$22.99
Fleetwood Mac
00690664 Best of......................$24.99
Flyleaf
00690870 Flyleaf......................$19.95
Foghat
00690986 Best of......................$22.99
Foo Fighters
00691024 Greatest Hits.............$24.99
00691115 Wasting Light............$24.99
Peter Frampton
00690842 Best of $22.99
Robben Ford
00690805 Best of......................$24.99
00120220 Guitar Anthology $29.99
Free
00694920 Best of......................$24.99
Rory Gallagher
00295410 Blues (Selections).....$24.99
Danny Gatton
00694807 88 Elmira St $24.99
Genesis
00690438 Guitar Anthology $24.99
Godsmack
00120167 Godsmack..................$19.95
00691048 The Oracle $22.99
Goo Goo Dolls
00690943 Greatest Hits Vol. 1...$24.99
Grateful Dead
00139460 Guitar Anthology $34.99

Green Day
00118259 ¡Tré! $21.99
00113073 ¡Uno! $21.99
Peter Green
00691190 Best of $24.99
Greta Van Fleet
00369065 The Battle at Garden's Gate $24.99
00287517 Anthem of the Peaceful Army..........$22.99
00287515 From the Fires...........$24.99
Patty Griffin
00690927 Children Running Through $19.95
Guns N' Roses
00690978 Chinese Democracy...$24.99
Buddy Guy
00691027 Anthology $24.99
00694854 Damn Right, I've Got the Blues............$19.95
Jim Hall
00690697 Best of $22.99
Ben Harper
00690840 Both Sides of the Gun .$19.95
00691018 Fight for Your Mind...$22.99
George Harrison
00694798 Anthology...................$24.99
Scott Henderson
00690841 Blues Guitar Collection$24.99
Jimi Hendrix
00692930 Are You Experienced?..$29.99
00692931 Axis: Bold As Love $24.99
00690304 Band of Gypsys..........$27.99
00690608 Blue Wild Angel........$24.95
00275044 Both Sides of the Sky .$22.99
00692932 Electric Ladyland.......$27.99
00690017 Live at Woodstock $29.99
00119619 People, Hell & Angels $27.99
00690602 Smash Hits $29.99
00691152 West Coast Seattle Boy (Anthology)........$29.99
00691332 Winterland $22.99
H.I.M.
00690843 Dark Light.................$19.95
Buddy Holly
00660029 Best of......................$24.99
John Lee Hooker
00690793 Anthology $29.99
Howlin' Wolf
00694905 Howlin' Wolf $22.99
Billy Idol
00690692 Very Best of..............$24.99
Imagine Dragons
00121961 Night Visions $22.99
Incubus
00690688 A Crow Left of the Murder....................$19.95
Iron Maiden
00690790 Anthology...................$27.99
00691058 The Final Frontier $22.99
00200446 Guitar Tab $34.99
Alan Jackson
00690730 Guitar Collection $29.99
Elmore James
00694938 Master of the Electric Slide Guitar ..$19.99
Jane's Addiction
00690652 Best of......................$24.99
Jethro Tull
00690684 Aqualung...................$24.99
00690693 Guitar Anthology $24.99
00691182 Stand Up $22.99

John 5
00690898 The Devil Knows My Name $22.95
00690814 Songs for Sanity $19.95
00690751 Vertigo $19.95

Eric Johnson
00694912 Ah Via Musicom $24.99
00690660 Best of $29.99
00691076 Up Close $22.99
00690169 Venus Isle $29.99

Robert Johnson
00690271 New Transcriptions $27.99

Janis Joplin
00699131 Best of $24.99

Judas Priest
00690427 Best of $24.99

Kansas
00690277 Best of $24.99

Phil Keaggy
00690911 Best of $24.99

Toby Keith
00690727 Guitar Collection $19.99

The Killers
00690910 Sam's Town $19.95

Killswitch Engage
00120814 Disarm the Descent $22.99

Albert King
00690504 Very Best of $24.99
00124869 In Session $24.99

B.B. King
00690492 Anthology $29.99
00130447 Live at the Regal $19.99
00690444 Riding with the King $24.99

Freddie King
00690134 Collection $22.99

Marcus King
00327968 El Dorado $22.99

Kiss
00690157 Alive! $19.99
00690356 Alive II $24.99
00694903 Best of $29.99
00690355 Destroyer $19.99
00291163 Very Best of $24.99

Mark Knopfler
00690164 Guitar Styles $27.99

Greg Koch
00345767 Best of $29.99

Korn
00690780 Greatest Hits Vol. 1 $24.99

Kris Kristofferson
00690377 Collection $22.99

Lamb of God
00690834 Ashes of the Wake $24.99
00691187 Resolution $22.99
00690875 Sacrament $24.99

Ray LaMontagne
00690977 Gossip in the Grain $19.99
00691057 God Willin' & The Creek Don't Rise $22.99

John Lennon
00690679 Guitar Collection $27.99

Linkin Park
00690922 Minutes to Midnight $22.99

The Lumineers
00114563 The Lumineers $22.99

George Lynch
00690525 Best of $29.99

Lynyrd Skynyrd
00690955 All-Time Greatest Hits $24.99
00694954 New Best of $24.99

Yngwie Malmsteen
00690577 Anthology $29.99

Marilyn Manson
00690754 Lest We Forget $22.99

Bob Marley
00694956 Legend $22.99
00694945 Songs of Freedom $29.99

Pat Martino
00139168 Guitar Anthology $29.99

John McLaughlin
00129105 Guitar Tab Anthology $27.99

Mastodon
00690989 Crack the Skye $24.99
00236690 Emperor of Sand $22.99
00691176 The Hunter $24.99
00137718 Once More 'Round the Sun $24.99

Andy McKee
00691942 Art of Motion $24.99
00691034 Joyland $19.99

Don McLean
00120080 Songbook $22.99

Megadeth
00694952 Countdown to Extinction $24.99
00691015 Endgame $27.99
00276065 Greatest Hits $27.99
00694951 Rust in Peace $27.99
00690011 Youthanasia $24.99

John Mellencamp
00690505 Guitar Collection $24.99

Metallica
00209876 Hardwired... To Self-Destruct $24.99

Pat Metheny
00690562 Bright Size Life $24.99
00691073 Day Trip/Tokyo Day Trip Live $22.99
00690646 One Quiet Night $24.99
00690559 Question & Answer $27.99
00690558 Trio 99-00 $24.99
00690561 Trio Live $27.99
00118836 Unity Band $22.99
00102590 What's It All About $24.99

Steve Miller Band
00690040 Young Hearts: Complete Greatest Hits $24.99

Ministry
00119338 Guitar Tab Collection $24.99

Wes Montgomery
00102591 Guitar Anthology $27.99

Gary Moore
00691092 Best of $27.99
00694802 Still Got the Blues $24.99

Alanis Morissette
00355456 Jagged Little Pill $22.99

Motion City Soundtrack
00691005 Best of $19.99

Mountain
00694958 Best of $22.99

Mumford & Sons
00691070 Sigh No More $22.99

Muse
00118196 The 2nd Law $19.99
00151195 Drones $19.99

My Morning Jacket
00690996 Collection $19.99

Matt Nathanson
00690984 Some Mad Hope $22.99

Night Ranger
00690883 Best of $19.99

Nirvana
00690611 Nirvana $24.99
00694895 Bleach $22.99
00694913 In Utero $22.99
00694883 Nevermind $19.99
00690026 Unplugged in New York $19.99

Nothing More
00265439 Guitar & Bass Tab Collection $24.99

The Offspring
00690807 Greatest Hits $24.99

Opeth
00243349 Best of $22.99

Roy Orbison
00691052 Black & White Night $22.99

Ozzy Osbourne
00694847 Best of $27.99

Brad Paisley
00690933 Best of $27.99
00690995 Play $29.99

Christopher Parkening
00690939 Solo Pieces $24.99

Les Paul
00690594 Best of $24.99

Pearl Jam
00694855 Ten $24.99

Periphery
00146043 Guitar Tab Collection $24.99

Carl Perkins
00690725 Best of $19.99

Tom Petty
00690499 Definitive Collection $24.99

Phish
00690176 Billy Breathes $24.99

Pink Floyd
00121933 Acoustic Collection $27.99
00690428 Dark Side of the Moon $22.99
00142677 The Endless River $19.99
00244637 Guitar Anthology $24.99
00239799 The Wall $27.99

Poison
00690789 Best of $22.99

Elvis Presley
00690299 King of Rock 'n' Roll $22.99

Prince
00690925 Very Best of $24.99

Queen
00690003 Classic Queen $24.99
00694975 Greatest Hits $27.99

Queens of the Stone Age
00254332 Villains $22.99

Queensryche
00690670 Very Best of $27.99

The Raconteurs
00690878 Broken Boy Soldiers $19.95

Radiohead
00109303 Guitar Anthology $29.99

Rage Against the Machine
00694910 Rage Against the Machine $24.99
00119834 Guitar Anthology $24.99

Rancid
00690179 And Out Come the Wolves $24.99

Ratt
00690426 Best of $24.99

Red Hot Chili Peppers
00690055 BloodSugarSexMagik $19.99
00690584 By the Way $24.99
00690379 Californication $22.99
00182634 The Getaway $24.99
00690673 Greatest Hits $24.99
00691166 I'm with You $22.99
00690255 Mother's Milk $24.99
00690090 One Hot Minute $22.95
00690852 Stadium Arcadium $29.99
00706518 Unlimited Loved $27.99

Jerry Reed
00694892 Guitar Style of $24.99

Django Reinhardt
00690511 Definitive Collection $24.99

Jimmie Rodgers
00690260 Guitar Collection $22.99

Rolling Stones
00690014 Exile on Main Street $24.99
00690631 Guitar Anthology $34.99
00694976 Some Girls $22.95
00690264 Tattoo You $19.95

Angelo Romero
00690974 Bella $19.99

David Lee Roth
00690685 Eat 'Em and Smile $24.99
00690942 Songs of Van Halen $19.95

Rush
00323854 The Spirit of Radio $22.99

Santana
00173534 Guitar Anthology $29.99
00690031 Greatest Hits $24.99

Joe Satriani
00276350 What Happens Next $24.99

Michael Schenker
00690796 Very Best of $24.99

Matt Schofield
00128870 Guitar Tab Collection $22.99

Scorpions
00690566 Best of $24.99

Bob Seger
00690604 Guitar Collection $24.99

Ed Sheeran
00234543 Divide $22.99
00138870 X $19.99

Kenny Wayne Shepherd
00690803 Best of $24.99
00151178 Ledbetter Heights $19.99

Shinedown
00692433 Amaryllis $22.99

Skillet
00122218 Rise $22.99

Slash
00691114 Guitar Anthology $34.99

Slayer
00690872 Christ Illusion $19.95
00690813 Guitar Collection $24.99

Slipknot
00690419 Slipknot $22.99
00690973 All Hope Is Gone $24.99

Smashing Pumpkins
00316982 Greatest Hits $24.99

Social Distortion
00690330 Live at the Roxy $24.99

Soundgarden
00690912 Guitar Anthology $24.99

Steely Dan
00120004 Best of $27.99

Steppenwolf
00694921 Best of $22.95

Mike Stern
00690655 Best of $27.99

Cat Stevens
14041588 Tea for the Tillerman $19.99

Rod Stewart
00690949 Guitar Anthology $19.99

Stone Temple Pilots
00322564 Thank You $26.99

Styx
00690520 Guitar Collection $22.99

Sublime
00120081 Sublime $22.99
00120122 40 oz. to Freedom $24.99
00690992 Robbin' the Hood $19.99

SUM 41
00690519 All Killer No Filler $19.95
00690929 Underclass Hero $19.95

Supertramp
00691072 Best of $24.99

Taylor Swift
00690994 Taylor Swift $22.99
00690993 Fearless $22.99
00115957 Red $21.99
00691063 Speak Now $22.99

System of a Down
00690531 Toxicity $19.99

James Taylor
00694824 Best of $22.99

Thin Lizzy
00694887 Best of $22.99

.38 Special
00690988 Guitar Anthology $22.99

Three Days Grace
00691039 Life Starts Now $22.99

Trans-Siberian Orchestra
00150209 Guitar Anthology $19.99

Merle Travis
00690233 Collection $24.99

Trivium
00253237 Guitar Tab Anthology $24.99
00123862 Vengeance Falls $24.99

Robin Trower
00690683 Bridge of Sighs $19.99

U2
00699191 Best of: 1980-1990 $24.99
00690732 Best of: 1990-2000 $29.99
00690894 18 Singles $27.99

Keith Urban
00124461 Guitar Anthology $29.99

Steve Vai
00690039 Alien Love Secrets $24.99
00690575 Alive in an Ultra World $22.95
00690172 Fire Garden $34.99
00156024 Guitar Anthology $39.99
00197570 Modern Primitive $29.99
00660137 Passion & Warfare $29.99
00690881 Real Illusions: Reflections $27.99
00690605 The Elusive Light and Sound, Vol. 1 $29.99
00694904 Sex and Religion $24.95
00110385 The Story of Light $24.99
00690392 The Ultra Zone $19.95

Van Halen
00700555 Van Halen $22.99
00295076 30 Classics $29.99
00700092 1984 $24.99
00700558 Fair Warning $24.99

Stevie Ray Vaughan
00690024 Couldn't Stand the Weather $22.99
00690116 Guitar Collection $29.99
00694879 In the Beginning $19.95
00660136 In Step $24.99
00660058 Lightnin' Blues 83-87 $29.99
00690550 Live at Montreux $29.99
00217455 Plays Slow Blues $24.99
00694835 The Sky Is Crying $24.99
00690025 Soul to Soul $19.95
00690015 Texas Flood $22.99

Volbeat
00109770 Guitar Collection $24.99
00121808 Outlaw Gentlemen & Shady Ladies $24.99

T-Bone Walker
00690132 Collection $22.99

Muddy Waters
00694789 Deep Blues $27.99

Doc Watson
00152161 Guitar Anthology $24.99

Weezer
00690071 The Blue Album $22.99
00691046 Rarities Edition $22.99

Paul Westerberg & The Replacements
00691036 Very Best of $19.99

The White Stripes
00237811 Greatest Hits $24.99

Whitesnake
00117511 Guitar Collection $24.99

The Who
00691941 Acoustic Guitar Collection $22.99
00690447 Best of $24.99

Wilco
00691006 Guitar Collection $24.99

The Yardbirds
00690596 Best of $24.99

Yes
00122303 Guitar Collection $24.99

Dwight Yoakam
00690916 Best of $22.99

Frank Zappa
00690507 Apostrophe $22.99
00690443 Hot Rats $22.99
00690624 One Size Fits All $27.99
00690623 Over-Nite Sensation $24.99

ZZ Top
00121684 Early Classics $27.99
00690589 Guitar Anthology $27.99
00690960 Guitar Classics $24.99

HAL•LEONARD®
Complete songlists and more at **www.halleonard.com**
Prices and availability subject to change without notice.

GUITAR *signature licks*

Signature Licks book/audio packs provide a step-by-step breakdown of "right from the record" riffs, licks, and solos so you can jam along with your favorite bands. They contain performance notes and an overview of each artist's or group's style, with note-for-note transcriptions in notes and tab. The online audio tracks feature full-band demos at both normal and slow speeds.

AC/DC
14041352.............................$24.99

AEROSMITH 1973-1979
00695106 ....$24.99

AEROSMITH 1979-1998
00695219 ....$22.95

DUANE ALLMAN
00696042.............................$24.99

BEST OF CHET ATKINS
00695752.............................$24.99

AVENGED SEVENFOLD
00696473.............................$24.99

THE BEATLES
00298845.............................$24.99

BEST OF THE BEATLES FOR ACOUSTIC GUITAR
00695453 ....$26.99

THE BEATLES HITS
00695049.............................$24.95

JEFF BECK
00696427.............................$24.99

BEST OF GEORGE BENSON
00695418.............................$24.99

BEST OF BLACK SABBATH
00695249.............................$24.99

BON JOVI
00696380.............................$22.99

ROY BUCHANAN
00696654 ....$22.99

KENNY BURRELL
00695830.............................$27.99

BEST OF CHARLIE CHRISTIAN
00695584.............................$24.99

BEST OF ERIC CLAPTON
00695038.............................$24.99

ERIC CLAPTON – FROM THE ALBUM UNPLUGGED
00695250.............................$24.99

THE DOORS
00695373 ....$22.95

DEEP PURPLE – GREATEST HITS
00695625.............................$24.99

DREAM THEATER
00111943 ....$27.99

ESSENTIAL JAZZ GUITAR
00695875 ....$19.99

FLEETWOOD MAC
00696416 ....$22.99

ROBBEN FORD
00695903 ....$22.95

BEST OF GRANT GREEN
00695747.............................$24.99

PETER GREEN
00145386.............................$24.99

BEST OF GUNS N' ROSES
00695183.............................$24.99

THE BEST OF BUDDY GUY
00695186 ....$22.99

JIM HALL
00695848 ....$29.99

JIMI HENDRIX
00696560.............................$27.99

JIMI HENDRIX – VOLUME 2
00695835 ....$24.99

JOHN LEE HOOKER
00695894.............................$24.99

BEST OF JAZZ GUITAR
00695586.............................$29.99

ERIC JOHNSON
00699317.............................$27.99

ROBERT JOHNSON
00695264.............................$24.99

BARNEY KESSEL
00696009.............................$24.99

THE ESSENTIAL ALBERT KING
00695713.............................$24.99

B.B. KING – BLUES LEGEND
00696039 ....$22.99

B.B. KING – THE DEFINITIVE COLLECTION
00695635 ....$22.99

MARK KNOPFLER
00695178.............................$24.99

LYNYRD SKYNYRD
00695872.............................$24.99

THE BEST OF YNGWIE MALMSTEEN
00695669 ....$24.99

BEST OF PAT MARTINO
00695632.............................$24.99

MEGADETH
00696421 ....$22.99

WES MONTGOMERY
00695387.............................$24.99

BEST OF NIRVANA
00695483.............................$24.95

VERY BEST OF OZZY OSBOURNE
00695431 ....$22.99

BRAD PAISLEY
00696379 ....$22.99

BEST OF JOE PASS
00695730.............................$24.99

TOM PETTY
00696021 ....$24.99

PINK FLOYD
00103659 ....$27.99

THE GUITARS OF ELVIS
00174800 ....$22.99

BEST OF QUEEN
00695097.............................$24.99

RADIOHEAD
00109304 ....$24.99

BEST OF RAGE AGAINST THE MACHINE
00695480.............................$24.99

JERRY REED
00118236 ....$22.99

BEST OF DJANGO REINHARDT
00695660.............................$27.99

BEST OF ROCK 'N' ROLL GUITAR
00695559.............................$24.99

BEST OF ROCKABILLY GUITAR
00695785.............................$22.99

BEST OF CARLOS SANTANA
00174664 ....$22.99

SLASH
00696576.............................$22.99

SLAYER
00121281.............................$22.99

BEST OF SOUTHERN ROCK
00695560.............................$19.95

STEELY DAN
00696015.............................$22.99

MIKE STERN
00695800.............................$27.99

BEST OF SURF GUITAR
00695822.............................$22.99

STEVE VAI
00673247.............................$24.99

STEVE VAI – ALIEN LOVE SECRETS: THE NAKED VAMPS
00695223.............................$27.99

STEVE VAI – FIRE GARDEN: THE NAKED VAMPS
00695166 ....$22.95

STEVE VAI – THE ULTRA ZONE: NAKED VAMPS
00695684 ....$22.95

VAN HALEN
00110227.............................$27.99

THE GUITAR STYLE OF STEVIE RAY VAUGHAN
00695155 ....$24.95

BEST OF THE VENTURES
00695772.............................$24.99

THE WHO – 2ND ED.
00695561 ....$22.95

JOHNNY WINTER
00695951 ....$24.99

YES
00113120 ....$24.99

BEST OF ZZ TOP
00695738.............................$24.99

HAL•LEONARD®

www.halleonard.com

COMPLETE DESCRIPTIONS AND SONGLISTS ONLINE!
Prices, contents and availability subject to change without notice.